Psychic Development

INTUITIVE
KNOWLEDGE

How to be Psychic Through
Visionary Clairvoyance

- **Simple Steps to Full Psychic Awareness**
- **Trigger Your Latent Clairvoyance**
- **Easy Visual Techniques for Quick Results**
- **Fascinating 'How to' Facts**
- **Make Your Own Unique Psychic Cards**
- **Essential Training for Psychics**
- **In-Depth and Interesting New Techniques**
- **Become Psychic as You Sleep**
- **First Steps to Becoming a Medium**
- **The Secrets Psychologists Don't Tell You**

CRAIG HAMILTON-PARKER

TESTIMONIALS

"I don't normally buy this stuff. I think it's odd and peculiar and you can't really put your finger on this kind of thing, however both these people everything they said about the stuff they talked about, they were accurate. They are the real deal and it kinda blew my mind a little bit. I'm not a mind blower by nature but you know it was real and all crap aside, it was real."

ERIC ROBERTS
(Talking to camera about his reading with Craig & Jane)

Eric Anthony Roberts is an American actor and brother of Julia Roberts. His career began with King of the Gypsies, earning a Golden Globe Award nomination for Best Actor Debut. He earned both a Golden Globe and Academy Award nomination for his supporting role in Runaway Train

"That was remarkable…In the World's Most Skeptical Person's Award in 2001 I was a runner up but I just don't know what to make of what I've just seen. I think he did remarkably well!"

CHRIS PACKHAM
(Talking on BBC 'Inside Out' about Craig's psychic demonstration)

Christopher Gary "Chris" Packham is an English television presenter.

"Craig is one of the most highly-respected spiritualists and mediums out there." **Weekly News**

"I'm overjoyed. To me this is proof that my father is there, somewhere. How else could Craig have known those things?... In fact, for one strange moment in the dim light, I almost believe it's my dad sitting there. I leave feeling buoyant and comforted. I find myself talking to my parents in my head. Thanks to Craig, I'm convinced they can hear me."
Journalist Amanda Ward - once skeptical journalist writing in **The Daily Express**.

"I'm Impressed!" – **Carol Vorderman** – on TV's *Put it to the Test*

"They really are psychic!" **Chris Evans** – Channel 4's *Big Breakfast* and BBC *Top Gear*

"The couple (Craig & Jane) are now the most talked about British celebrities… and foremost psychic television stars. One of their most memorable television appearances was talking with princess Diana from beyond the grave."
Francine Hornberger in her book *The World's Greatest Psychics*

Craig & Jane Hamilton-Parker
Psychic Mediums

CRAIG HAMILTON-PARKER

Contents:

PART 3

Dictionary of symbols and images

PART 4

Bonus Chapter: Developing Mediumship

What can you see in these images?

The pictures you see come from your subconscious mind and will contain psychic messages about your life and the future.

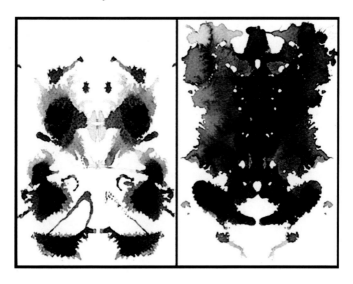

An example of the inkblot Intuition Cards you will make and use for some of the psychic exercises in this book

TRIGGER YOUR VISIONARY CLAIRVOYANCE

When a newbie joins one of my psychic development circles I often get them started by using the simple visual projection techniques that I describe in this book. They can be undertaken alone or with other people. Although easy to understand and practice they are nonetheless also very powerful and for some people these techniques become something they use throughout their psychic career. Using these tested techniques you will not only awaken your latent psychic abilities but will also gain insight into traditional divination methods such as fire reading, sand geomancy, cloud divination and using the crystal ball. You will take your first steps towards telepathy and ESP – Extra Sensory Perception – and make a start at psychometry, mediumship and spirit communication. I have written other best-selling books that carry on from where this book leaves off but if you are an absolute beginner this book is a great starting point. Advanced Mediumistic teachers may also find this book of benefit with lots of get-you-started techniques that make for fascinating metaphysical workshops and development circles.

Your first steps into the psychic world will naturally be hesitant and you'll be worried about getting things wrong and making a fool of yourself. Everyone feels like this at the start for it's a big leap from thinking you are psychic to actually practicing psychic skills and finding out for certain if you really have the gift. I hope that my book will also give you reassurance and confidence by showing you how initially you can work on yourself to access your subconscious mind and then gradually practice your gifts with others.

The first step is to connect to your everyday intuition and I will show you how you can get answers to questions immediately from your subconscious mind. I then demonstrate how you can amplify and enhanced these insights so that not only does your subconscious give you answers but your latent clairvoyance begins to work through you as well. Your sixth sense feeds information to you though your subconscious mind and will give you amazing insights that bypass your rational skeptical mind. You will learn to visually project the information arising from your intuition and your clairvoyance. Once you can verify and trust the strange information that your psychic awareness is giving you, your abilities will soon flower. You will instantaneously have intuitive knowledge about people, the future, the past and you will come to understand that everyone has natural psychic abilities that can be activated once you know the techniques. Using amusing and easy to practice techniques I will show you how to unlock your intuition and then reveal more advanced methods that will allow your clairvoyance to flow.

When we first start out it is very hard for the student to work without any aids so the methods I have devised here begin by using Rorschach ink blots to act as an objective and visual mirror to your subconscious mind. This is a powerful psychological method that opens the hidden world of the subconscious mind and I have adapted and modified the Swiss psychologist Hermann Rorschach's method to reveal the secrets of the sixth sense also.

You'll be shocked at how soon you gain access to your inner world and how quickly you find your psychic abilities awaken. Although this is a recognized psychological projective method it originated from a much more ancient tradition that may go back to the Neolithic times. You will learn to look at random shapes and discover pictures, images and faces that can be interpreted as either psychological symbols or psychic insights.

PART 1

YOUR HIDDEN POWERS OF THE INTUITION

When you were a small child you would have seen extraordinary pictures in the clouds that seemed to have a magical quality. Although many adults may consider this as just a fanciful waste of time it is in fact harking back to a natural psychic method that connects us to the spiritual forces around us. Our ancient ancestors used this and other forgotten methods to awaken naturally the psychic skills that were once part of everyday life and taken for granted. Once you have awoken your natural archaic senses I will show you modern psychological dream techniques and spiritual techniques to take you further along the path towards full psychic development and mediumship. By reconnecting with your ancient powers you will find that you can become the source of incredible psychic insights.

Simple Steps to Full Psychic Awareness

All our interior world is reality — and that perhaps more so than our apparent world.
Marc Chagall

According to the dictionary[1] intuition is 'immediate mental apprehension without reasoning; immediate insight.' It's something that we all take for granted, yet is it not remarkable that somehow we can come to correct conclusions without having all the facts to hand and without using reason? How is it that we can form an immediate assessment of a person the first time we meet them and find that our initial insight is proved to be correct. And why is it that we can sometimes make a correct guess at a direction to travel or guess the answer to a question and get it exactly right? What is it that gives us these immediate insights?

---

[1] Collins (London & Glasgow)

Behind our normal consciousness lies the vast untapped world of the subconscious. Here, are locked away billions of memories and incredible skills that we never use. Every one of us is a secret genius. The subconscious is capable of amazing creativity, inventiveness and mental agility. For example, experiments with hypnosis have shown that it is possible to remember just about anything. Things that are impossible to remember normally, such as what you had for lunch on May 14th 2004, can be recalled with perfect clarity during hypnotic trance. All of this knowledge is locked away in the subconscious and can be utilized if we allow our intuition to do its job. The intuition is something we all have. For most people it remains a mysterious force that works when we least expect it.

One of the functions of this book is to enable you to get in touch with these psychological powers and to help you make the best of your creative faculties. It will also help train your intuition so that you can use it in everyday situations. In addition, the methods can be used to help you come to terms with the emotional side of yourself. You will be shown initially how to use ink blots and other techniques to find creative solutions to problems, stimulate ideas and give you insight into your dreams and the subconscious processes of the psyche. You will even discover how the intuition can be developed to put you in touch with the psychic side of yourself and your higher spiritual self.

Your Hidden Powers of the Intuition

Imagination is the eye of the soul
Joseph Joubert

In order to become attuned to the intuition you will need to become more aware of the psychological forces that lie below the surface of the conscious mind. You must listen to your inner voice, trust your hunches and pay careful attention to the content of your dreams. If you do this you will become in harmony with yourself and unlock creative powers that you never realized you had.

BECOME PSYCHIC AS YOU SLEEP

The hidden power of intuition often reveals itself in dreams. The intuition is at work while we sleep and can sometimes offer solutions to problems through dreams. During the day your subconscious mind may have noticed something about a person or a situation and will bring this to your attention through a dream. For example, you meet a friend, then that evening have a dream about their being ill. You noticed nothing wrong with them. However your subconscious may have observed telltale signs of an illness. The tone of the complexion, an imperceptible odor, a slight quiver in the voice—all these subtle signals may be subconsciously observed and then brought to your attention during sleep when the intuition is allowed to function.

PROBLEM SOLVER

In many cases the intuition gives us an answer to a problem or provides us with information that it is impossible to know. The most obvious of these is if we have an intuitive glimpse of the future. There are thousands of documented examples of precognition and clairvoyance. For example, there are cases on record of people who have dreamed of disasters such as the Chernobyl nuclear accident or had a premonition that Princess Diana would die. Others have claimed to have dreamed of a winning horse or found the correct location of a lost object through a dream or by a sudden intuitive insight while awake.

SPONTANEOUS INTUITION

As you work with this book, pay careful attention to the way your intuition functions in everyday life. Do you listen to your hunches and trust those gut feelings? The intuition needs to become part of your life and not just something you work with every time you open this book. From today, observe your intuitive feelings about people or situations. Perhaps you could even keep a notebook to log the spontaneous first impressions you get. Later you can check these to see just how accurate your intuition can be.

Intuitive Discoveries

Genius, in truth, means little more than the faculty of perceiving in an unhabitual way.
William James

Some of the greatest minds trusted their intuition to help them solve some of the most difficult intellectual problems. Sometimes the best way to deal with a problem or solve a problem is simply to 'sleep on it'. During the day the conscious rational mind is in complete control of our life and we do things because there's a logical reason for behaving in such a way. However at night the intuition and psychic insights break through the stranglehold of reason and forces an idea upon us that we could never have arrived at by logical thought alone. The intuition is the source of many great ideas.

Many great inventions are the result of intuition. For example, the sewing machine owes its invention to a dream. Elias Howe was stuck for a solution for a working model. One night he dreamed that a savage king ordered him to invent a sewing machine. When Howe said that he'd tried but couldn't, the whole tribe raised their spears to kill him. Just before the fateful moment, Howe noticed that each spear had a hole in it just above the point. This was the vital clue needed for the commercial perfection of the sewing machine.

Atomic physics owes one of its fundamental discoveries to the intuitive insight of a dream. Neils Bohr was trying to understand the nature of the atom. One night he dreamed of a sun composed of burning gasses with planets orbiting it attached to fine threads. When he awoke he realized that this was the solution to his puzzle. It explained the structure of the atom and heralded the birth of atomic physics.

There are, of course, many examples of spontaneous insight the have come because of a sudden intuitive understanding. This Eureka effect has influenced inventors, generals, artists, scientists and people from just about every profession. The truth is that the subconscious is like an incredible inner computer that continues to solve problems for us in the background of our normal awareness. When it has done its work, the answers pop into our head. Similarly, the subconscious can interrupt our conscious thinking and make an instantaneous assessment of a situation. It may note something about a person's tone of voice or body language and warns us that this person is not quite what they seem. This is why our gut feelings about people so often prove correct. In short, intuitive people listen to the wisdom and prompting from the subconscious. If you want to be psychic, you must first become intuitive.

The intuition and ESP

If you can look into the seeds of time and say, which grain will grow, and which will not, speak then to me. **Shakespeare.**

It is through the intuition that we can also access the powers of Extra Sensory Perception – a term coined by the scientist Joseph Banks Rhine and a subject that we will study in detail later in this book. Extra sensory perception (ESP) refers to any mental faculty which allows a person to acquire information about the world without the use of the known senses. It is broken down into the categories listed below:

Telepathy: *the ability to 'tune in' to the thoughts of others or to inject your own thoughts into another's mind.* If you know who's calling before you answer the phone then you may have picked up the other persons thoughts. Telepathy takes no notice of distance. Your friend could be calling from Australia and you'd still pick up the mental signals. Edgar D Mitchell, the astronaut on board Apollo 14, even conducted a telepathy experiment with a 'sender' on earth as he winged his way to the moon!

Clairvoyance: *the power to see things that aren't available to you by the known senses and aren't known by anyone else.* Some people have an amazing sense of direction and can find their way around without maps or signs. They just 'know' which way to go. There are also people who can sense water either by dowsing with rods or by holding their hands over maps. Perhaps you've helped someone find a missing object and suddenly had a hunch as to where it is and been proved right? You may be using clairvoyance to get this information.

Precognition: *the skill of looking into the future and seeing events before they take place.* Your intuitive gifts may have given you a hunch about a winning horse or even guessed the winning numbers of the lottery. For example a man from Portsmouth UK knew he was going to win the lottery the day before he took part. He even announced it to all his friends. The next day he bought a scratch card and won £50,000!!

Psychokinesis: *the ability to use the power of the mind to influence matter — to move objects by thought, for example.* You may think that there's no way you have this power but have you noticed how machinery breaks down when you're angry or upset? The telephone goes "on the blink" during an argument or the fax machine jams as soon as there's a deadline. You may be influencing your environment with your psychic energy.

Unlocking the Subconscious.

The sky is the daily bread of the eyes.
Ralph Waldo Emerson

There are many ways to access the intuition. In particular, play and imagination bring us close to this creative source. A creative pursuit such as painting, sculpture or music can put us in touch with the intuition. When you deal with people, your intuitive self-forms subconscious judgements based on subliminal perception of facial expression or voice tone. This is particularly apparent between mother and child. How do you know that your baby is about to wake or that he is disturbed when with the baby sitter? It is because the intuition has access to information brought through supersensitive perceptions or even paranormal insight.

As a child you probably gazed at white cumulus clouds drifting in the blue sky and noticed how they form into the fantastic shapes of faces, animals and spectacular landscapes. These changing images come from the subconscious and are projected by the mind onto the random cloud shapes. The pictures formed reveal the hidden processes from deep within you and the thoughts being generated by your innermost self. It's a form of daydreaming and, just like the symbols in a dream, the pictures are keys that reveal the hidden secrets of the mind

The pictures you see are a reflection of what is happening in your subconscious and can reveal a great deal about your hopes, fears and feelings. In addition, psychic people claim that, just like dreams, these symbolic images can occasionally contain messages about the future. Shortly before his death in 1977, Elvis Presley stood gazing into the sky above Gracelands. He looked sullen and worried and is said to have confided in his friends that he could see his own death forecast in the clouds passing by.

Gazing at clouds is an ancient form of divination to predict the future called Nephelomancy and such things as the color, direction it moves, position in the sky and the shape of the cloud formations all had special significance to the ancients. The sun, stars and the sky have always been considered the realm of the gods and, to the seers of old, the mysterious shapes were direct messages from the gods. Many ancient and tribal cultures give prayers and libations to the clouds for an angry sky god may send destructive storms or floods bring drought with no rain at all. These people were looking for symbolic messages about the weather as well as omens for the future of their personal life.

Human history was changed when the Roman Emperor Constantine, days before the battle of Milvian Bridge on 28 October 312, saw the sign of a cross made of light in the clouds that sat above the sun and had the inscription, "By this symbol you will conquer." He gazed at it in wonder as his whole army witnessed the miracle. When night came he dreamed of Christ who told him to carry the sign of the cross on his standards and into battle. It was a resounding victory and the battle marked the beginning of Constantine's conversion to Christianity. If he hadn't have seen the cloud vision and converted, then Christianity would have never spread across the world in the way it did.

Now I am not saying you should start having religious visions but the above stories illustrate how cloud gazing and similar techniques are part of an ancient tradition, formed the basis of many modern divination techniques and are a sure fire way to help you access your intuition. If you gaze at any random pattern, you are likely soon to see faces and pictures in its haphazard form. Many people claim that they can see a face in the shadows of Mars or in the patterns on the moon's surface. Similarly, you may notice that when you look at the coals of a fire, the patterns in sand, a rock formation or the gnarled bark of a tree, pictures are revealed in their shapes. Psychics use random shapes such as tea leaves, hot coals, smoke patterns or the flaws in a crystal ball to project the images from their intuition.

If you would like to give this technique a try you will need to choose a day in which there is enough contrast between the blue sky and the clouds to allow for shapes to form. Cumulus clouds against a blue sky or the orange skies of the setting sun are the easiest clouds to work with. A gentle wind also adds interest and changes the shapes so that multiple images can be interpreted as a symbolic sequence of prophecies. It's not essential but, if it's a nice day and the grass is dry, lie on the ground. Remember that these initial techniques I am showing you are just a taster of psychic and divination ability so tread lightly and approach things with a serious but also a cheerful state of mind. Do not use this method when you feel depressed or have life changing issues to resolve.

To begin a cloud reading you must have a clear question in your mind. Do not ask about silly or frivolous things just to test it. If you approach this with respect you are more likely to get a sensible answer to your question in the images that appear. Once you are comfortably positioned, close your eyes and allow distracting thoughts to subside. Enter a peaceful and relaxed state of awareness. Allow your question to become clear in your mind and, when you feel fully relaxed and focused, open your eyes and allow yourself to be drawn to the cloud shapes. The pictures you see in the clouds reflect what is happening in your subconscious mind and will give a symbolic answer to the question you have asked.

Sometimes the cloud shapes will have nothing to do with your question and you will most likely see many distorted faces and sometimes alarming images. What you are trying to do is allow your intuition to help you. You are better to allow your mind to enter a state of dreamy revelry so that what you see is a gentle unfoldment of your subconscious feelings. Be patient and relaxed as the images appear and now look to your feelings to see if the images you are seeing reflect your emotional associations with the questions you have asked. You will not necessarily get a definitive answer but allowing your feelings and thoughts to project themselves onto the clouds will bring you closer to your real feelings, hopes and fears. You already have the answer within you but now you are letting it appear to your conscious mind.

The images are symbols of how you are feeling and, if your latent clairvoyance has come into play, may also hint at events in the future. Remember that symbols are malleable and can have more than one meaning so don't just latch onto good or bad images but examine your intuitive feelings to see if you can understand the answer to your question.

You are seeing these pictures because your intuition is at work and trying to create an order out of randomness. What you see is your subconscious mind mirrored on the clouds. And if we can 'see' the subconscious mind then we can be aware of our innermost thoughts and feelings and act upon them. If you interpret any of these images as symbols of the future, use common sense: Anyone who has interpreted the Tarot cards will know how careful you have to be when death images are revealed in the cards. Similarly, with cloud reading, death images are symbols and not necessarily portents of a real death. We usually interpret death images as the death of the old so that the new can emerge. At New Year we have the symbol of Old Father Time who, just like the "grim reaper," carries a scythe. The past year is cut down so that the new one can begin. Death images therefore can be very positive symbols in a cloud reading.

Psychologists use a similar visual projection technique when they ask their patients to look at a

Rorschach Ink Blot—a subject which we will be looking at later in the book. From these random shapes they interpret what they see as representations of the patient's hidden needs, hopes and fears. In ancient times, the seers went a stage further: They believed that the pictures seen in fire embers, clouds, Nature and even in the entrails of sacrificial animals represent auguries and portents for the future. In the clouds they would read about the shape of things to come.

Get into the habit of seeing pictures in random shapes. You can be really serious about it or simply start off by enjoying it as a game to see who can see the most pictures in the clouds, in a coal fire or in the trees when walking through the woods.

As an aside here's another simple, amusing experiment that you can try. Psychokinesis (PK) is the scientific term for the mind's ability to influence matter. An intriguing PK experiment that you can try with clouds is to exercise your powers to influence their shape. In 1956 Dr Rolf Alexander, a London physician, demonstrated, in a public test, his ability to change cloud shapes by thought. Skeptical journalists watched him concentrate on a three-cloud group. His plan was to maintain the position of the two smaller clouds while dispelling the third large one. To everyone's amazement the smaller clouds increased in size and the big one became smaller. It really does work. Try it yourself.

Philosophy and the intuition

There are no facts, only interpretations.
Fredrich Nietzche

The mystics and the scientists have differing views about what the intuition is and how it works. It will inevitably be a subject of debate because most intuitive experiences are subjective and not repeatable in the laboratory. What appears as an amazing hunch, could just be clever guesswork. Theories have been put forward to say that, in ancient times, successful societies used intuition in favor or reason. For example, Robert Graves in *The White Goddess* argues that intellect is a comparatively recent discovery. The first people were intuitive rather than intellectual: magical rather than scientific. Man only developed the intellect to increase the speed and efficiency of his material development. One day the two systems— reason and intuition—will unite to form something more powerful than either.

Some scientists, psychologists and philosophers have attempted to reduce the intuitive process to a psychological function and have proposed that intuition is the brain's capacity for subconscious computation. Others consider it to be the result of collective learned habits and social conditioning. There are also theories put forward by biologists proposing that intuition is part of our biological instinct, for example, the intuition of a salmon in locating its spawning ground.

Philosophers have also attempted to explain what intuition is. Immanuel Kant maintained that it is through intuition that we construct and maintain the basic elements of our world. He claimed that our sense of space and time, our sense of identity, our sense of beauty and goodness, and our sense of the truth of things are all founded on our intuitive understanding.

Philosophy says that intuition is prior to all perception and all reasoning. It is the function that enables us to comprehend and understand the world. Similarly, in linguistics, intuition is considered as the process by which listeners recognize the meaning of words and sentences. Intuition is the quality that brings everything together. It may be the case that we are born with a certain amount of intuitive knowledge. For example, developmental psychologists have documented the existence of both spatial awareness and "innate grammar" in infants, before they could have learnt these things from social conditioning.

All of these ideas are valuable but they still do not explain the mysterious nature of intuition and its apparent paranormal abilities. Clearly, the word 'intuition' means many different things to different people.

Are you intuitive?

Think about the ways intuition is used in your everyday life. Take your time thinking about the questions that follow and identify the nature of your intuitive powers. The more you think about your intuitive self, the more these psychological powers will emerge within you.

1. **What words or phrases would you use to define intuition?** Perhaps you would describe it as "knowing" without being able to explain how you know. Or you may choose words to describe intuition such as: a gut feeling; insight; a hunch; seeing or hearing something that "leapt out" or "came out of the blue" or perhaps you had a "flash" of inspiration. Think of the specific occasions that you have used these terms.

2. **Can you remember an intuitive experience that happened to you?** Perhaps you can recall an insight that 'came out of nowhere'. Think about what your first impressions were when you first met people you know now. Were these 'gut feelings later proved to be true or did you misjudge people. Ask yourself whether you truly had an intuitive insight. Or were you reacting from prejudice or perhaps had preconceived opinions about the person.

3. **In what type of situation does your intuition work best?** Perhaps you are a good judge of character and quickly get intuitive insights about the people you meet? Maybe you get hunches at work? Do you perhaps get your best intuitive material when working on creative projects? Maybe you are good at pre-empting children's needs?

4. **Do you trust your intuition?** How do you feel when you make a decision based upon your intuition? Perhaps you think it's foolish to be so rash? Many people feel confident when they obey the prompting of their "inner voice" or follow what their heart tells them. Are there any occasions when you should have trusted your intuition?

Perhaps you can think of times when your intuition was completely wrong?

5. **What motivates your intuition?** For some people the intuition is a protective force that warns when a situation is dangerous or you are in danger of being tricked by someone. Has your intuition seen through a lie? Perhaps your intuition is like a conscience that guides you or is it influenced by guilt? Are there aspects of yourself that you repress that can sometimes be misinterpreted as a spiritual prompting?

6. **What senses do you use with your intuition?** Do you see a picture in your mind's eye? Perhaps you hear an inner voice. Some people get a nasty metallic taste in their mouth when they are warned by their intuition. Does your intuition work through your emotions? Perhaps you notice some change in your bodily functions like a rise in temperature or shakiness in the limbs when your intuition is at work.

7. **Have you ever had psychic intuition?** Perhaps you dreamed of the future or know who's on the other end of the telephone before you answer it. When you were at school, did you know that some of your schoolmates would do well in life and you

were proved correct? Or perhaps you have felt that a terrible tragedy would befall someone and it proved to be true.

Hermann Rorschach (1884-1922)

Hermann Rorschach was born on November 8, 1884 in Zurich, Switzerland. His father was a painter and he considered the same career before opting to study psychiatry at Eugen Bleuler's clinic in Zurich.

While working in a Swiss psychiatric hospital with adolescents, he noticed that certain children gave characteristically different answers to a popular game known as Blotto (Klecksographie). The game of Blotto involved looking at inkblots to see who could see the most interesting pictures in the random shapes. It struck Rorschach that what the children were seeing revealed a great deal about their psychological condition. From this simple game, he devised the Rorschach Test, which today is considered as one of the best psychodiagnostic procedures and an indispensable tool of psychiatry. In 1921, he published his ideas in his book *Psychodiagnostik*.

Hermann Rorschach himself never experienced any success with it. He had difficulties finding a publisher, and it was not well received when it finally came out. Today it is considered one of the great classics of psychiatry. Rorschach died of appendicitis in 1922 at the age of 37. He had only invested just under four years in his inkblot test, which has become perhaps the single most powerful psychometric instrument ever envisioned.

The Rorschach-Test

By the 1930's, there was a widespread interest in the Rorschach techniques, both in Europe and the USA. Unfortunately, there was also a great deal of controversy about how best to use the cards, and different schools evolved with sometimes diametrically opposed ideas. The European schools, guided by Ewald Bohm, tried to keep as closely as possible to Rorschach's original concept but in America the cards were being used in a great number of different ways. Eventually in 1960, John E Exner pioneered an alternative system, which is a synthesis of all these different systems. The Exner School is now the dominant methodology.

In spirit, Bohm's and Exner's systems are very similar. Both use complicated scoring systems and specific interpretations for each shape and area of the inkblots. To understand and apply the Rorschach systems takes considerable training and expertise. You will appreciate that methods taught here, the cards used, and the objectives of the techniques employed, are completely different from those of Rorschach and his successors. You will be using the free-flow of your imagination to trigger your intuitive and psychic abilities whereas the psychologists working with specifically designed ink-blots were using them for specific therapeutic reasons. For example on some of the cards the ink is red, which some patients will identify with blood. Responses to them can provide indications about how a subject is likely to manage feelings of anger or physical harm. This card can induce a variety of sexual responses. Similarly there's an ink blot that looks just like a woman's vagina and another that looks like tall man with a huge penis! These ink blots may encourage talk about sex and the threatening male figure may trigger ideas such as the patient's view of authority figures and so on. In some ways it could be argued that the psychologists are cheating as there's a hidden agenda and the patient is being directed to talk about issues that have not necessarily arisen spontaneously from their subconscious.

The cards used by psychiatrists are printed from the original plates, which are now 75 years old. Each reprinting requires great attention, and is made on what can now only be regarded as ancient equipment. However, this ensures that the prints are virtually an identical reproduction of the originals. Even the weather is taken into account. If it is too humid, or too dry, the printing process is rescheduled.

Understanding the subconscious.

Hermann Rorschach was not the first person to use inkblots as a psychological tool. Leonardo da Vinci and Justinus Kerner used inkblots as to inspire creative thinking. However, the Rorschach method gives an empirical method to interpret the images and shapes seen in each card that can be used to assess the psychological condition of a patient. Many psychologists interpret the images and symbols seen as products of the *subconscious*.

LEVELS OF THE MIND

Sigmund Freud (1856–1939) coined the term *psychoanalysis* to describe his methods for curing the mental problems of his patients. He believed that most of these were caused by sexual difficulties that were repressed into areas of the mind that we are unaware of. He used the analogy of an iceberg floating in water to describe this hidden part of us.

The top 1/7th that pokes above the surface of the water represents our conscious mind. It is the conscious awareness we have when we are awake. The surface of the water itself is the boundary between the conscious mind and the subconscious mind—represented by the section of the iceberg below the water. Freud called this the Pre-Conscious and it contains material accessible to the conscious mind such as facts, memories, ideas and motives. This part of the mind disguises the information coming from the subconscious by changing it into symbolism so that we will not be disturbed by what our subconscious is really thinking.

Below the Pre-Conscious lies the largest part of the mind, which Freud called the *Personal Subconscious*. This 6/7ths contains our secret wishes and fears as well as the traumatic memories of the past. It stores repressed traumas and emotions and unacknowledged motives and urges. It is the uncontrolled instinctive side of us. Freud believed that the subconscious thoughts are completely hidden and unavailable to us.

The Archetypes and the Collective Subconscious.

Between 1907 and 1913 Freud's star pupil, Carl Gustav Jung, fell out with Freud and proposed a new theory of the subconscious. Freud had recognized that the subconscious could retain 'daily residues'—images from our daily life that had been forgotten. But Jung noticed that some of his patients were expressing themselves with imagery from ancient traditions. He wondered if the subconscious could hold ancient or *'archaic residues.'* Jung's patients were using inherited imagery harking back to forgotten mythologies buried in the subconscious.

In 1919 Jung called these images *archetypes.* Furthermore he proposed that we have a *collective subconscious* which is formed of the instincts and the archetypes. The archetypes are inborn forms of intuition which are the necessary determinants of all psychic processes. They manifest as images. They are like primordial ideas and are numinous, electrically charged with a sense of the sacred. Many of the images you will see in the cards are archetypal symbols originating from the collective subconscious. They are powerful symbols that represent the innermost processes within your psyche.

The origins of projective oracles

For some people their intuition is so powerful that it causes them to hallucinate. They may see images and pictures from their subconscious projected into the world around them. It is very common for this to happen on awakening from a dream. Many clairvoyants and psychics use these visual projection techniques as a method for accessing their psychic powers. The best known of these techniques is Crystallomancy— crystal ball gazing.

The Mayans, Incas, North American Indians, Australian aborigines and many tribal societies throughout the world used crystal-gazing. It came to Europe in about the fifth century and was a very popular pursuit during the Victorian era. And of course, today there is a massive resurgence in interest in crystals, crystal healing and crystal gazing.

The Crystal Ball

The crystal ball is the classic tool of the clairvoyant. Many occultists believe it is the oldest method of precognition, existing even before the invention of writing. Today people still use the same techniques to induce visions as they did centuries ago. The practitioner makes his mind as blank as possible and gazes into the center of the crystal. As he does, the crystal may appear to go milky and out of this white blur will emerge scenes, images and faces. Sometimes these pictures are static like a photograph and sometimes they are dynamic, appearing as though you were watching a miniature television.

By carefully noting what is seen the clairvoyant will interpret the images as either glimpses of the future or as a way of getting better acquainted with the subconscious mind. Sometimes these techniques can reveal startling facts about the future. Just as with the pictures you saw in the clouds when you were a child, crystal gazing is a way of accessing the subconscious mind by projecting imagery onto a form.

Crystal gazing is a type of scrying—a form of divination by gazing into a reflective surface. Likewise, the techniques you will learn with the intuition cards are also a form of scrying but a lot easier to master than the crystal ball. Instead of projecting the imagery from the subconscious onto the formless glass of the crystal, the inkblots easily take on the shapes and pictures that the psychic intuition is trying to reveal.

Scrying and Scryers

Scrying is perhaps the most accurate form of prediction there is. It was used by most of the great seers whose predictions have stood the test of time. Often it was used in conjunction with astrology. Crystal gazing has links with hydromancy — divination by water — because water and other liquids were once the only reflective material available to most people. Often sacred pools or springs were used as well as fonts or bowls of 'holy' water. It is known that the Babylonians gazed into bowls of water to divine the future; the Egyptians used a pool of ink held in the hand and the Hindus gazed at bowls of molasses. Again these methods took advantage of the mind's ability to project the images from the subconscious onto a surface or into a clear or reflective materials.

When most people think of a crystal ball gazer they think of gypsy fortune-tellers or wild eyed women in turbans. This is the stereotypical image that has been propagated in the popular press, movies and the media. But some of the best seers of all time have worked with the crystal ball and similar items. Dr John Dee, astrologer to Queen Elizabeth

1st, used a crystal egg and a black obsidian mirror to make his prophecies, and Nostradamus gazed into a brass bowl of water on a tripod next to a lit candle to make his prophecies.

If you want to try this technique you need to apply a similar methodology to what you learnt with cloud gazing. This is a form of what is called scrying, which is the practice of looking into a translucent ball, smooth surface or other reflective material such as water or crystals to see spiritual visions. It was not originally used as a form of fortune-telling. The visions that come when one stares into the glass come from the subconscious and activated imagination but, as I have explained, this is also the part of the mind to which the sixth-sense brings its information. In the past, people also believed that the images were brought by gods, spirits and devils. In my own experience I have found it is not a reliable way to do mediumship.

When you look into a crystal ball it acts as a focus for the attention. Just as chanting a mantra or gazing into a candle fixes the attention, the crystal ball stops the conscious mind from holding control and allows the intuitive mind to flow into the screen of your attention. You are entering a light trance state but will have full control of your faculties and can stop at any point.

Once you are in a lucid, relaxed state of mind—a sort of relaxed revelry as I described with cloud watching—you may see images appearing in the reflections within the crystal ball. It is best not to leap mentally at everything you see but to try to maintain a relaxed and flowing state of mind. It's important also not to stare hard but to gaze gently. If your eyes start to strain or water then stop.

If all goes well and you can maintain a relaxed and open state of mind, you may see a rich pageant of visual images and dramatic stories that seem to be projected within the glass itself. This is what psychics and mediums call objective clairvoyance in that you are seeing your visions outside of yourself. It is just as valid to see these images directly within your mind's eye, which will be something like experiencing an inner movie. From the flow of images you may 'see' events and people that will be important to you now or in the future. In this case I have suggested that you simply look into your crystal ball and allow whatever wants to appear, appear. You can, if you wish, ask a question as we did before looking at the clouds, and interpret the images you see as symbolic answers.

Nostradamus

Perhaps the most famous seer to use scrying to prophesy was Michel de Notredame (1503-1566) — better known to most people as Nostradamus. Although Nostradamus explains his predictions by astrology, most of his prophecies were obtained by scrying and then dated afterwards using astrology. His prophecies included the Great Fire of London in 1666, the French Revolution, Napoleon's defeat at Waterloo, the nuclear bombs at Hiroshima and Nagasaki and many more harrowing predictions yet to come.

The technique Nostradamus used was to gaze into a bowl of water resting on a brass tripod. He called this his 'magic mirror'. Here, in the candle-lit waters he would see visions of the future, which he then wrote in quatrains (four line verses) in a mixture of Old French and Latin. To add to the mystery perhaps, and protect him from the potential persecution of the church, he then coded his work. He would add words of his own invention, substitute names with initials, introduce nicknames and finally fill his work with puns and anagrams.

John Dee

One of the strangest scryers was John Dee (1527-1608)—an acclaimed mathematician and astrologer to Mary Tudor. With the help of Edward Kelly, he used scrying in combination with a complicated system of numbers to communicate with the angels. According to Dee, an angel would appear in the center of the crystal ball. She would then point in sequence to numbers and letters on a chart. Dee called the language of these communications *'Enochian'* and published is his three volume diaries *Quinti Libri Mysteriorum*[2]. Of course, many sceptics have said that all this is nonsense and fantasy but find it difficult to explain the strange fact that the 'Enochian' language has a consistent grammar and syntax.

The intuition cards can be used in a similar way to the methods of Nostradamus and Dee. They are a means by which you can access the supernormal powers of the subconscious and, in the right hands, may reveal the secrets of destiny.

---

[2] Sloane MS. 3188 in the British Library

Visual projection

For many people, scrying and crystal gazing are very difficult methods to master. It is uncomfortable to sit, with watering eyes, gazing into glass or crystal. For most, there are no results after months of patient sitting. It is not known why some people get results using scrying and others struggle hopelessly. It is estimated that only about one person in 20 is psychically sensitive enough to get results with this method. Some psychologists have pointed out that this ability has nothing to do with psychic powers at all. Crystal gazing is only a way of inducing visual hallucinations similar to the hypnagogic imagery that some people see between sleeping and waking. Psychics argue that the imagery is generated by the subconscious, which also contains the clairvoyant faculty of the mind.

Not everybody can tap the subconscious or clairvoyant powers by scrying with water, crystal, glass or mirrors. However most people can see a face or pictures in crumpled clothes, clouds or a blot of ink. As a child you may have found it easy to see pictures and shapes in the things around you. As you became an adult this ability may have become lost. Learning to see the world again through a child's eyes is hard as our reason holds such an iron grip upon our world that the magic of the imagination suffocates.

Deliberate visual projection in order to access the intuitive powers is very different from the uncontrolled hallucinations of mental illness. In the latter case the patient loses touch with reality. They fail to distinguish between imagery and perception and suppose that what they imagine is external and can be seen by others. Children sometimes fail to make the distinction as do people who are in solitary confinement, isolation or as a response to intense emotional need. Hallucinations evaporate when the person realizes that others do not see the world as they do.

Shakespeare expresses the nature of a hallucination perfectly in his play, *Macbeth*. While planning to kill Duncan, Macbeth hallucinated a dagger: "Art thou not, fatal vision, sensible to feeling as to sight? Or art thou but a dagger of the mind, a false creation, proceeding from the heat-oppressed brain?"

Macbeth had lost touch with reality. With the intuition cards you can use the power of visual hallucination while keeping your feet firmly on the ground. You will learn to use the incredible powers of the subconscious without being deceived by hallucination. Seers and prophets have safely used these techniques that use the mind's ability to project visually the subconscious contents for centuries.

Fire Oracles

One of the first oracles to take advantage of the mind's ability to form pictures from random shapes was pyromancy—the art of divination from fire. It is thought that this divination technique may have originated in Neolithic times, and possibly right back to when fire was first discovered, and was the earliest form of divination. It is believed that in Greek society, virgins at the Temple of Athena in Athens regularly practiced pyromancy as well as followers of Hephaestus, the Greek god of fire and the forge. In Renaissance magic, pyromancy was classified as one of the seven "forbidden arts," along with necromancy (raising the dead), geomancy (reading sand, earth and landscapes), aeromancy (cloud and weather reading), hydromancy (water divination), chiromancy (palmistry), and spatulamancy (Divination of the shoulder blades).

In ancient times pyromancy was used when

sacrifices and burnt offerings were made to the gods. The ancient seers would study the flames as the sacrifices were made and from them interpret auguries and omens. For example, a clear flame burning without smoke or sound was considered a sign of good fortune. The way the smoke rose, its smell and its thickness were all considered being messages from the gods. In addition, other methods of divination at the sacrificial pyre included divination from burning leaves, divination from objects cast into the fire and the sounds made by casting salt or laurel leaves into the fire. Seers with prognostic vision would chant mantras and spells, gaze deep into the flames and see in there elemental spirits and salamanders that would give them messages about the future.

Visual projection techniques were used by the shaman seers as a means of stimulating clairvoyance and knowledge of the future. Many of these old techniques still survive and it is still possible in some Arab countries and India to employ a pyromancer to foretell the future. The technique involves sitting quietly in front of a fire that has died down to a bed of glowing coals and entering a state of relaxed meditation. When the pyromancer is ready, ritual dictates that he should then scatter a handful of salt upon the glowing coals. Once the flames and crackling have died down, he gazes into the fire and contemplates the pictures he sees in the glowing shapes in the coals for between 10 and 15 minutes.

How to Read Fire

A number of different pictures may appear but one should stand out from the rest as being particularly significant. If no image is seen, then the pyromancy is abandoned and a new fire lit in 24 hours' time. However, if one shape stands out clearly then this is considered to be important and is interpreted as the oracle for the future. It is considered particularly auspicious if the coals glow for this brings great good fortune.

Once the symbol from the fire has been determined, it is interpreted according to a set of traditional meanings. For example, a windmill will represent a change for the better, as will a fountain, but to see flowers in the coals bodes disappointment. However the true clairvoyant would see beyond these traditional meanings and listen to the voice of his intuition to elicit the true meaning of the omen. From this inner prompting, it is hoped he will gain a true and accurate precognition.

If you want to try this yourself you can use a method similar to the way you read the clouds or the crystal ball. Your state of mind is what's most important. Again I recommend you get into a relaxed, cheerful and dreamy state of mind and simply allow your imagination to play with the shapes its sees. These you can interpret as symbols for your situation or for someone else if you ask a question on their behalf.

Pyromancy is also used in magical rituals and ceremonies to bring about fortuitous events. I have done some of these ceremonies with the yogis in India and it has achieved its desired results. In one instance we threw sacred herbs onto a fire and chanted mantras to help someone who was seriously ill back home in England. Within a few days they got better.

Another ancient technique is coal gazing. Write a question about the future on a piece of paper and, when the fire has become quiet and has glowing coals, place the paper face down on the top. Now look again into the embers and allow your mind to interpret the images you see in the glowing coals.

THE EVOLUTION OF ORACLES

There's an enormous variety of oracles that use random patterns and shapes to tell the future. For example, a popular love oracle involved interpreting the shapes made when egg white is dropped into a glass of water. Oenomancy predicted from the patterns made by wine poured out as an offering to the gods; Scapulomancy predicted from the patterns of cracks and fissures on the burned shoulder blade of an animal and Tephromancy predicted from the ashes of burnt offerings. Even the famous Chinese oracle called the *I Ching* originates from the ancient tortoise shell oracle that predicted from the cracks in heated tortoise shells.

Tasseography

Tasseography—tealeaf reading to you and me—is a popular technique used to access the intuition by using random patterns. Again, it is the pictures created by the shapes of the leaves that are interpreted as oracles for the future. This method of divination is thought to have come from ancient China, although the Romans used a similar technique to read the lees of their wine. In fact, the pattern made by the sediment left in the bottom of any drinking cup has always been interpreted to be of great importance in predicting the drinker's future. I know a fortune-teller who predicts the future by reading dirty plates! Again, the method is the same as for the traditional methods—he looks for pictures and interprets these as symbols for the future.

As with cloud reading and the technique of reading random patterns in inkblots that you will learn later, tealeaf reading is a highly subjective method of fortune telling that taps into the images generated by our subconscious mind. One person may see a group of leaves as one thing and another will see something completely different. You are the person who is likely to recognize a symbol that relates to the matters surrounding whoever has asked the leaves a question and therefore the most qualified to interpret the meanings of the symbols.

Geomancy

The ancient art of geomancy is also experiencing a revival. This is divination by interpreting the signs and symbols from the earth. In Tibet, it was customary for the travelling monk to interpret oracles from the shapes and forms he encountered in the landscape. The pictures seen in the shape of rocks, or in the mountain's melting ice, all augured for the future. Sometimes matters of state would be decided according to the omens seen in the simulacra observed in rocks, trees or in the stains in walls of temples. Similarly, in Christian countries much controversy has centered on images of Christ that have appeared in the stains on flagstones or plaster walls. Today, clairvoyants read the pictures and shapes in a tray of sand as a means of focusing clairvoyance.

You now understand what lies at the heart of the techniques employed with visual projection onto random shapes. The powers of the mind to project visual images into clear water, the crystal ball, or random patterns, gives us direct access to the subconscious mind. On one level these powers can be used to tell us about the processes going on in the subconscious mind; on another they help us to unlock the powers of extrasensory perception and enable us to divine the future.

Psychic Inkblot Experiment

Random patterns found in tea leaves, clouds, or the patterns formed in a crumpled sheet of paper act as a sounding board for the mind to project images from your subconscious mind. This ability of the mind to see images—and particularly faces—in random shapes is called Pareidolia, which is a psychological phenomenon wherein the mind perceives a familiar pattern of something where none actually exists. The mind wants to understand the world around us so tries to make sense out of random patterns and so turns them into all sorts of strange and wonderful pictures. We have been using this odd ability of the mind to gain access to our own hidden thinking process but also to our subconscious psychic abilities.

Having read so far in this book, you might, by now, have tried some of the methods I have described on your friends. Now I am going to help you make a set of ink blots that are reminiscent of the Rorschach ink blots used by psychologists. Psychologists use them to access the repressed and hidden urges in the subconscious but we are going to use them to access our psychic abilities and eventually to give someone an intuitive psychic reading.

I will now describe how to make one ink blot on paper that can be used to give a reading. Later I will suggest you make a series of these ink blots and make them into a set of cards that you can use to give readings or use as a tool for reflective meditation. It's a messy job so you may want to try just one to get started and have a go at making up a set of cards later. The cards can be as large or as small as you like. Ask a friend or family member — basically someone who is quite sympathetic to your cause — to sit with you, and give them a reading. Explain to them that this is just a simple psychic experiment and you're going to have a go and see what you get. Ideally it would be best to have a sympathetic sitter that you nothing about, so that your reading is not influenced by things you already know about them.

Making your ink blot cards

Step 1. You will need white paper, black ink, an artist's paintbrush, and water. This experiment can be messy so use plenty of old newspapers to protect your table and/or carpets. Divide everyone into pairs. One person will read and the other will be read.

Step 2. Using a paintbrush, put some drops of water and drops of black ink onto a sheet of paper. Now fold the paper in half so that the water and ink merge to form shapes and tones in a symmetrical pattern — just as you may have done in school to create "butterflies." Allow it a few minutes to dry.

Step 3. Relax as you look at the inkblot. Let your imagination discover pictures in the shapes. It is likely that the first things you will notice in the swirls of ink are faces and figures. Ask yourself what emotions these faces symbolize: Are they happy, sad, perplexed, angry, contemplative, or whatever? The mood expressed by the face may symbolize how the sitter has been feeling. Describe what you see to your recipient and discuss it if it relates to the way he or she has been feeling recently.

Step 4: Once you are accustomed to seeing pictures, you will eventually notice more subtle images. Look not only in the black areas but in the white areas too. See what pictures are formed there— much like a negative image. Look at the overall shape, but if you look closely you will also see pictures in the edges of the shapes and in the small details of the inkblot. The images that are most important are the ones you feel most drawn to, for it is your psychic intuition that is bringing your attention to them.

Step 5: Describe the images you see and what they mean to you. Explain what you believe this is saying about the person sitting in front of you. Say what you feel without trying to change it or over-rationalize. The pictures are symbols, so explain what you feel they represent. If you know a little about the meanings of dream symbols you can apply some of this knowledge. For example, if you see a bird you could interpret this as the sitter's desire to escape a problem, or perhaps it represents a desire to attain higher knowledge or freedom. A bird flying away from the nest may indicate someone leaving home or taking the plunge in a new enterprise. Or maybe the image is literal: The sitter may keep birds! Symbols are fluid things and there is no set interpretation. Use your intuition rather than logic to discover and explain what is meaningful to the sitter.

Step 6: Work with the images to see if there are other hidden meanings. Help the sitter to understand what issues are important and give some clear and sensible advice about how they can make the best of things. Perhaps you can gain insight into material you could not possibly know, such as stories from the sitter's childhood, his or her interests, hopes, and failures in life, and so on. Ask if the sitter can verify the information now coming from your psychic insights.

Step 7: When you have finished, ask the sitter how he or she felt about the reading and if the symbols meant anything different to him or her. The sitter may want to talk about some of the problems you identified, and you may want to give a little advice. Empower the sitter to deal with the issues rather than make predictions.

In a moment I will take you again through this inkblot reading process in a little more detail.

Studying the projected imagery that arises from the subconscious is a quick way of accessing your latent powers. Similar psychic aids include sand reading, in which the random patterns found in a tray of sand are interpreted, and scrying techniques such as gazing into a crystal ball, mirror, hearth fire, bowl of water, or black ink. Each of these psychic tools acts as a focus for the attention while the intuitive mind unfolds.

PART 2

WORKING WITH INKBLOT CARDS

As you have seen, cumulus clouds, hot coals, tea leaves and other random shapes can all be used as a mirror for the imagination, the subconscious and clairvoyance. By interpreting the pictures seen as symbols we understand what our intuition is telling us. The many pictures that you will see in its form are the keys to unlocking your psychic and psychological powers. I suggest you now make up a set of inkblots, as you did before, as a set of cards. I will be showing you some layouts and spreads you can try as a way to give simple readings. You could perhaps use half a sheet of paper for each card. (A5 or Junior Legal)

Another advantage to this inkblot technique is that people do not find these handmade cards intimidating as they would Tarot Cards and, as it all looks like fun, they are less inclined to be judgmental if you get things wrong. BUT when you do some practice in advance and CAN get things right it will most definitely blow their minds!

FACES AND CHARACTERS

Hold the cards and examine them. Already you may notice how the shapes of the ink form into pictures. You will probably just see faces at first, as these are the most common shapes that the mind imposes on the random swirls of ink. Some of the faces may be weird looking or distorted. They may be frightening, bizarre or funny. Sometimes the whole inkblot can form a face but, when your attention shifts, you may notice that what you thought was one face is made up of many other faces. Sometimes faces merge together or appear to interact or be part of a theatrical scene or situation. Enjoy watching the many interesting pictures emerge from the cards.

ANIMALS, BIRDS, INSECTS AND FISH.

If you look more closely and allow your imagination to roam you will see many other interesting pictures. Creatures are the second most commonly seen pictures in the cards. You may see cats, horses, pigs, butterflies, birds and even mythological beasts such as dragons, phoenixes and unicorns. At this stage don't worry about the symbolic meaning of your visions—just enjoy the process of allowing your imagination to awaken. This in itself is very therapeutic.

LANDSCAPES AND SCENES

As your thinking becomes more fluid, you may start to see all sorts of interesting landscapes and scenes. You may see castles and fantasy landscapes or industrial scenes, houses, rivers and forests. Allow your imagination to play and see how it creates increasing exotic environments. Gradually other pictures may emerge: boats, windmills, rings, towers, flowers, and so on. Everybody will see something different and each picture says something about you.

IMPROVING YOUR ABILITY TO SEE PICTURES

Some people find it easier to see pictures in random shapes and immediately can see pictures the moment they look at a card. For others, it takes a little work but, with practice, the pictures will soon start unfolding like a movie. To help you improve your ability to 'see', here are a few useful tips:

LOOK AT THE WHITE SPACES

As well as looking for pictures in the black ink, also look at the shapes made by the white areas. A white area surrounded by black ink may easily form into a negative silhouette of a picture. Also, look at the areas where the white and the black areas meet. At these contours, you may see how the outline of the black ink forms pictures. But also look at the white shapes at these places and see how the line draws familiar shapes. Now let your attention jump between the shapes you see in the black areas and the shapes in the white ones.

LOOK AT THE DETAILS

The overall shape of the inkblot may create a picture such as a face or a butterfly but it is possible to see pictures in any part of the inkblot. Try looking at small areas of the card to see what shapes and pictures are there. Once your imagination is activated, you will be able to see images in even the smallest detail of the card.

LOOK AT THE SUBTLE TONES

The subtle washes in the white and grey areas of the cards are one of the best areas to focus the attention. These 'cloud like' areas can reveal very detailed images that you may initially have missed. Hidden in the stains are some of the most interesting images.

TURN THE CARD AROUND

Once you've had a good look at the card try turning it upside down or to the side. You will notice that you are now confronted with all sorts of new shapes and completely different pictures are revealed. This fresh look at the cards can stimulate new images very quickly.

LET IT HAPPEN NATURALLY

The key to seeing lots of images is to enjoy what you are doing. Try playing the 'blotto' game with children to see who can identify and describe the most pictures. Also, try working with other random shapes. Look at the clouds or the gnarled bark of trees for strange faces and shapes. See what pictures reveal themselves when you look at the patterns in sand or in a pile of crumpled clothes.

PREPARING TO USE THE CARDS

A little preparation will greatly increase your ability to use the cards and enable you to gain the full benefit. Accessing the intuition is easy if you get yourself into the right frame of mind. You need to be relaxed yet alert. Just as the intuitive powers spontaneously manifest during sleep or in meditation so the following simple technique will help you get close to these states of consciousness as you use the cards.

Step 1. Prepare your environment.

Set aside a special time to work with the cards and choose somewhere where you will not be disturbed or distracted by noise. As part of your ritual you may want to light a candle and some incense to set the contemplative mood. Also, choose a comfortable chair or sit on the floor propped up by cushions. Get yourself as comfortable as possible.

Step 2. Breathe Deeply

This is one of the easiest ways to relax. As you take in a deep breath, think to yourself "I AM" then, as you breathe out, think to yourself "RELAXED". As you breathe out allow your whole body to completely relax. Sink into the pleasure of being so completely at ease.

Step 3. Deeply Relax

Now imagine the feeling of relaxation spreading through your whole body. Imagine a warm sensation in your toes and feet that spreads upward, relieving all stress. You may notice how your shoulders become relaxed and how all the pressures fall away—particularly around the eyes. Deeply relax. And feel how good it is.

Step 4. Imaginative Meditation

Once you are completely relaxed you will notice how the mind slows down and becomes at ease. Let go of all worries and notice how the imagination is beginning to activate. You may see pictures and images arising in your 'mind's eye'. Allow the moving images to come and go. Now draw them towards you and let them become exceptionally vivid. Try not to fall asleep but remain in this state between waking and sleeping. The more you relax, the more vivid the images become. It's like dreaming, but you are wide-awake.

Step 5. Coming around

Remain in this visionary state for as long as you wish. When you feel ready, bring yourself back to normal awareness. However, allow this fluid state of awareness to permeate your waking consciousness. Your imagination is now active, you are more in tune with your subconscious and your intuition is ready to work.

OPENING THE IMAGINATION

Now you are going to work with the intuition cards in a targeted way. The objective of this exercise is to ask the intuition to give you a symbol that may reveal some helpful guidance about your life in general. At this stage, it's best not to get too serious. Start with an open question and a good frame of mind. I suggest that you avoid cataclysmic questions such as 'Should I leave my partner?' or 'Should I hand my notice in tomorrow?' Indeed, it is sensible always to keep your questions open-ended. The objective is to understand what your intuition is telling you. Once you know this, you must then use your mental discrimination to decide if this is a sensible option.

EXPERIMENT TO OPEN THE INTUITION

Step 1. Once you have completed the exercise on the previous pages, select one of the cards drawn randomly from the pack. Again, close your eyes and relax for a few moments. Feel the breath quieten down.

Step 2. Hold the card in front of you or prop it up in front of you if you prefer to sit in a meditation posture. Let the imagination become active. Allow your thoughts to wander yet keep bringing them back to the card. Watch the pictures and images appear and disappear in the inkblots.

Step 3. Don't try too hard. Let the mind drift and allow the pictures to form spontaneously. Look at the shapes made by the inkblot but also observe the negative shapes made by the white paper. Turn the page upside-down or sideways and see what other shapes are formed. Look for the images you see in the smallest details of the inkblot.

Step 4. It may help to gaze at the page and watch what appears as your eyes go out of focus.

Step 5. After a while, one or two images are likely to seem the more dominant than others. Decide which ones these are and now make a note of the pictures that seem most relevant.

Step 6. The images you have been given are symbols of how you feel and what you should do.

In the next section, you will learn how to interpret these symbols using our symbol dictionary and your own skills of interpretation.

HOW TO UNDERSTAND PSYCHIC SYMBOLS

In the experiment, your intuition, by way of the cards, gave you some images. These images are symbols that have arisen from the subconscious. They express your feelings, your hopes and also your fears. By understanding the secret meaning of these given symbols you can discover more about yourself and find new ways to approach your situation. The symbols you have received are insights that come directly from your intuition. Now comes the job of understanding what they say about you.

WHAT DID YOU SEE?

Interpreting the images you see in the cards is a similar process to interpreting the symbols of a dream. Both come from your subconscious mind and give insight into the hidden aspects of you. For example, you are likely to have seen a number of faces in the cards. A face is the most common image that the mind will make from a random shape.

What was the face like? Was it happy, sad, fearsome, confused—or maybe it looked angry? The expression on the face may be saying something about your current state of mind or may say something about the attitude of the people around you. If you see an angry face then you may harbor hidden feelings of resentment towards someone or something. A confused looking face may illustrate how confused you are at the moment whereas a tranquil face can show the attitude you have or should be striving to achieve.

In the same way, consider every image you see and ask yourself what it says about you. Supposing you see an anchor: an anchor stops a ship drifting with the tide. We call people who support us an anchor. If our life feels like it is drifting aimlessly we need an anchor to hold us steady, such as a partner, a job, a home. It's clearly a symbol of stability, although of course it could say that you might want to travel by sea.

Animals are also a likely image you may have seen in the inkblots. Again ask yourself what they symbolize about you. A dog, for example, may represent an actual dog as well as those qualities of friendship, domesticity and loyalty. A ferocious dog could symbolize your fears or uncontrolled instincts. Interpret each image as a metaphor for your life.

In part 3 are listed some common symbols and their meaning. These represent only a rough guide. It is most important to interpret the images in your own way in order to understand the unique personal messages given to you by your intuition.

LEVELS OF MEANING

Symbols are a universal language that teaches and preserves permanent basic truths. They are a form of shorthand for ideas and concepts. This is especially true of religious concepts that have preserved their philosophies and protected them from enemies by translating them into symbols. Symbols continue to have a very powerful effect upon us. They can touch the depths of our being and put us in touch with the fundamental human values that should govern our life. Symbols connect us with the divine part of ourselves, the part that knows all the answers to the problems we face and the lessons we have to learn from life.

Earlier you read about how the mind is a fourfold hierarchy consisting of the *conscious mind*, the *preconscious*, the *personal subconscious* and *the collective subconscious*. The first three levels were proposed by Freud, while the forth was added by Jung. I have also added what I call the *transcendent subconscious* to include the information that you receive from beyond the mind by paranormal means.

Level 1. The Conscious mind.

Images that have come from the conscious mind are those that you are likely to have imposed upon the inkblot. For example, you may not like a picture you see and consciously try to change it into something else. Or you will only look at the obvious shapes and ignore the more subtle images that leap out when you give your imagination free reign. Consciously imposed images do not come from the intuitive mind but may say a great deal about you: why do you try to change an image into what you would prefer it to be? What are you avoiding?

Level 2. Preconscious and Personal Subconscious.

Many of the symbols that appear on the cards represent your own personal problems, hopes, wishes and fears. Occasionally what the pictures reveal may remind you of past hurts, childhood worries or repressed feelings. You may be shocked by what you see in the cards. You may see violent scenes, explicitly sexual scenes or scenes of pain and despair. Do not be alarmed by these. Symbols often exaggerate the truth in order to bring aspects of yourself that you are unaware of to your conscious attention. However, by recognizing these subconscious forces you are taking the first steps to solving your inner problems and worries

Level 3. Collective Subconscious and Transcendent Subconscious

From the deepest levels of the subconscious we receive images that help us to find the means to heal ourselves and solve our problems. You may see images in the cards that show you how to correct your behavior in some way or offer advance warnings of emotional tensions that may soon get out of hand. On a deeper level still, the images that arise may come from the divine, transcendent part of you. The visions that the cards capture come from the highest source and will leave you feeling mentally and spiritually inspired. Some of these symbols may reflect the way that you are preparing yourself for clairvoyance and spiritual revelation.

THE MEANING OF PERSONAL SYMBOLS

There are many symbols that we have in common, which occur in myths, dreams, religions and cultures from all over the world. However, symbols are also flexible and can mean different things to different people. They are your unique experience. To understand what a given symbol means to you, it is important to work with it and allow it to reveal its meaning. Your personal associations with the symbol are more relevant than the traditional meanings.

Ask yourself these questions:

What does the symbol say about me? Most of the pictures you see in the cards represent aspects of yourself. For example, supposing you see a crying face—this may mean that you are crying inside. Perhaps you have emotional worries that are upsetting you more than you dare admit.

What feelings do I associate with the symbol? As well as analyzing the symbol, notice how it makes you feel. Your emotional response to it may reveal a great deal about your present state of mind. The symbol may represent your emotional condition and highlight feelings that need to be expressed.

Is the symbol a pun? The subconscious will often use a play on words to express an idea. Supposing you see a shape in the cards that resembles a bottle of wine? Perhaps this is a pun to say that you are winging and whining too much.

Will the symbol talk to you? An imaginary dialogue with the symbol will help to reveal its meaning. Supposing you see the image of a horse: close your eyes and imagine that the horse can talk. Now see yourself asking it for its meaning. In your imagination let the horse tell you what it symbolizes. This fantasy technique can be used with most images to establish a dialogue with your given symbol. The trees, stones, faces and animals will talk to you and reveal their meaning.

Does the symbol remind you of something from the past? Perhaps the events you are experiencing now remind you of similar feelings from similar situations in the past. You may have happy or sad memories. Your intuition is giving you a symbol that helps you understand your true feelings about a person or a situation.

Programming the Subconscious to Solve Problems

For this next experiment, we are going to program

the intuition to answer a question. We are not going to ask for specific 'yes' or 'no' answers but are going to encourage the intuition to generate symbols and images to help you find a practical solution to your problems. You are about to draw upon the incredible creative power of the subconscious.

The intuition is like an incredibly powerful biological computer that we have forgotten how to use. Most people panic when they have problems. Problems create more problems and soon life is so complicated that you do not know how to deal with your difficulties. The inner computer overheats as you frantically punch the 'help' button. Clearly, the intuition cannot do its job in these conditions.

In order to program the intuition to answer questions, you must first disentangle yourself from your worries and calm down. Give yourself permission to stop worrying. Let go of your emotional attachment to your problems. Relax and keep it simple. Now identify just one issue that is troubling you and deal with this one first.

How to Ask the Question.

The way you word your question is important as

your subconscious will respond accordingly. For example, you may be worried about whether you should change your job and want to ask about this. However, in the 'back of your mind' are other concerns: a drop in wages may cause money problems; the job may entail moving; you may need to retrain etc. Clearly, a question such as "Should I take the new job?" may not get a clear answer. The job may be fine if you don't mind moving but may also cause financial difficulties etc.

A better question would be less specific. You may want to ask: "Tell me about my true feelings about changing jobs and what do I really want to do?" At this stage, we are asking the intuition to help us analyze our motives. First, we must know in our heart what we really want from life before we can devise practical methods to achieve the goal. Write down your question and now try the experiment on the next two pages.

Problem Solving Experiment

STEP 1. Prepare yourself

Close your eyes and relax. You may want to relax very deeply and let go of all stress. Notice how the breath slows down and your mind becomes quieter. Feel the relaxation spread upwards through your body, relieving all stress. Deeply relax, more and more and notice how good you are starting to feel. Let the shoulders relax and especially note how the tension around the eyes falls away. Let your mind float in that wonderful state between sleeping and wakefulness. Your mind is fluid yet you are fully alert.

STEP 2. Choose a card

Still retaining your relaxed state of awareness, open your eyes and randomly draw a card from the pack. Your intuition is already preparing answers to the question you've asked. Now look at the card and see the pictures emerge. Remember to look for both the shapes within the white areas as well as within the inkblot itself. Allow yourself to enter the dream like state that you practiced in the first experiment. Let go. Relax. Enjoy your fluid state of awareness.

STEP 3. Watch the images emerge

At first, don't worry about trying to remember or interpret the symbolism of the images. Let them emerge naturally and unimpeded. After about 5 minutes, or whenever you feel ready, make a few notes about what you saw. You are likely to have seen faces. Make a note of these but also make a note of the animals, scenes and other pictures you saw. Also, jot down any associations that come to mind with each picture. And, don't forget to include the good and bad feelings the images inspired.

STEP 4. Interpreting the symbolism

The images you have noted can now be interpreted in the same way you would interpret a dream. They are messages from your intuition that reveal your true feelings, hopes fears and motivations. What do these symbols say about the issue you've asked about? How does this session make you feel? Are your thoughts focused on the question initially asked or are you now thinking about something else? Perhaps you have overlooked something? Is your subconscious alerting you to other areas of your life that needs your attention? You may want to reread pages 42-47 to help you unravel the meaning of the symbols or you can read some of the common meanings from page 42. However, it is your interpretation that counts. Let your intuition guide you to the true meaning of the symbols you have seen. They are a visual manifestation of your inner voice.

STEP 5. Put it into practice.

A grain of practice is worth a mountain of talk. Write down a sentence or an affirmation that you feel sums up what your intuition is telling you. You may want to jot down a few keywords that may act as memory joggers for the days ahead. From now on start integrating what you have been given by your intuition into your life. Again, you do not necessarily have to make sweeping changes. Little changes, applied with persistent perseverance, are the most effective way to achieve a permanent improvement in your circumstances.

The Cards and Dreams

One of the best ways to deal with a problem is to 'sleep on it'. During sleep, our intuition is at work solving our problems and offering us solutions to those problems. Dreams are the intuition's way of communicating with our conscious self by using the language of symbols, metaphor and allegory. If you can understand the meaning of your dreams, it will help you to improve yourself by identifying your motives, strengths and weaknesses. Dreams can help you to solve a wide range of psychological and practical problems. The cards will give you insight into the meaning of your dreams.

THE CARDS AS A DREAM MIRROR

If you work regularly with the intuition cards, your dreams will naturally become more vivid and alive. This is because you are making a conscious effort to discover the hidden processes that are happening within you. You are now more attuned to the subconscious part of yourself. Your dreams continue your work with the inkblot experiments and continue solving your problems as you sleep.

Sometimes when you look at the cards, you may be reminded of dreams you have had. Similarly, you may dream about something associated with some of the pictures you saw in the card experiments. Dreams and the cards are both doorways to the subconscious and to the wisdom that comes through the intuition. When you sit and watch the images come and go in the cards you are in effect dreaming while wide-awake. The cards are dream mirrors. What you see in the cards is a dream unfolding and, just like a real dream, it will give you insight into yourself.

DREAM SYMBOLS

Dreams can be a form of self-expression. Their symbols say a great deal about you and the way you feel. For example, if you dream about being chased this may represent how you are running away from a problem. It may illustrate how you refuse to face up to something about yourself or your circumstances. Similarly, if you dream of falling this may indicate that you are anxious and feel that you have lost your sense of equilibrium and balance in life. The dreams say that your situation is *like* falling or *like* running away.

In the same way, the scenarios expressed by the pictures you see in the cards draw parallels to the way you feel about your life. When you are given an image compare it with some of the dreams you may have had. If you regularly note down your dreams in a dream diary, you may want to compare them with the images you have been receiving through the cards. If you note similarities, consider why certain images keep recurring. What do they say about you and the way you are feeling now?

Both the cards and your dreams draw upon the powers of the subconscious. Working with the cards as well as with your dreams will give you insight into yourself and help you make the best decisions about the issues that affect your life. Dreams, of course, also contain many prophecies for the future so working in this way will help you to develop your ability of precognition—seeing the future.

REMEMBERING YOUR DREAMS

Dreams can be infuriatingly difficult to recall. Sometimes just a half-remembered snippet is recalled or you only remember the dream you had on awakening but forget all the dreams from throughout the night. Many people have great difficulty in recalling any dreams although scientists have demonstrated that everyone dreams every single night. The best way to remember a dream is to keep a notepad beside your bed and write your thoughts down immediately you wake up. If you do this every morning, you will soon be recalling your dreams.

You probably only occasionally recall a dream but with a little effort you can ensure that you remember your dreams every morning. These dreams can be interpreted and used as part of your spiritual work. The intuition cards can help you to remember your dreams:

DREAM EXPERIMENT

Step 1. Preparation. Put the cards, a notepad and pen beside your bed before you retire. Make sure that you have something to lean on and adequate light so that it is easy to make notes as soon as you wake up. The decision that you want to have a dream increases the likelihood that you will remember a dream when you wake up. As you get ready to go to sleep, say to yourself "Tonight I will remember my dreams."

Step 2. Immediate Recall. If you wake up and remember a dream, write it down immediately. Write down any words you remember and things that were said in the dream first, as verbal information from dreams is most easily forgotten. Don't worry about grammar or the order of events—just try to get as much material onto the paper as you can.

Step 3. Gradual Recall. If you wake up to find that you cannot remember a dream, then lie in the same position for a while and allow yourself to drift between sleeping and wakefulness. Continue to relax and allow your mind to 'float'. This will give your intuition a chance to draw a dream to your attention. Do not think about the events ahead and start planning today's 'to do' list. Allow a dream to come.

Step 4. Use the cards for recall. If you remember

nothing at all about your dream, reach for the cards. Continue to keep your attention on the objective of remembering your dreams and remain in a state as close to sleep as possible. Now look at the cards and allow the pictures to form. You will notice that the pictures come more easily when you are in a sleepy state. Don't worry about trying to interpret any of the images you see, we are looking for pictures to jog your memory.

Step 5. Let the cards speak to you. As the pictures form you will be reminded of similar pictures from your dream. The cards will act as a sounding board and the images revealed will be very close to those found in your last dream. The more you allow your imagination to work with the cards, the more of the dream you will remember.

Step 6. Dig deeper. Even if you were fortunate enough to have immediate recall, there may still be many details that you missed. Look at the cards and think about the dream you have just had. Do new pictures jump out of the page? Do they remind you of anything else from your dream? The pictures you see in the cards will act as catalysts to help you remember all of the dreams you had that night.

USING THE CARDS FOR CREATIVITY

Anyone who works in a creative profession will know that there are times when the ideas just don't come. Often these blocks happen at the worst possible time such as when there's a copy or design deadline to meet. You need an idea, a good one, and you need it now! The more pressure that's put on you the harder it becomes to come up with a creative solution. Fortunately there are simple ways in which the cards can help you get into the right state of mind that is favorable for creative thinking.

USING THE CARDS TO OVERCOME CREATIVE BLOCKS

The best ideas come to us when we least expect them to. We may wake up in the morning with a brilliant idea or something may come to us when we are driving a car or doing the washing up. It's often when we temporarily stop worrying about a problem, such as when our mind is distracted by a banal task, that our intuition is able to give us the ideas that we've been struggling to find.

Often the best solution is to put the problem aside

for a while and let the subconscious mind continue working in the background. Once its work is done, it will wait for the right opportunity and then pop the answer into your head.

The cards can be used to create this opening. On the next pages you will use the cards as part of your creative thinking processes. By taking time out to work with them we give ourselves a temporary respite—an emotional holiday in which we can enjoy a contemplative state of mind. It's at this time that the intuition can communicate with the conscious mind.

Half the battle in overcoming creative or intuitive blocks is to break the routine tension of your thinking. You could achieve similar results if you took a short stroll or spent more time looking at the glorious beauty of nature. However, if you work in an advertising agency, research and development department, newspaper or design house it is unlikely that the boss would appreciate your absence. In these situations the cards can be used as a necessary distraction to get you into a more contemplative state. You will be able quickly to achieve a relaxed and fluid state of mind that is essential for creative thinking.

EXPERIMENT WITH CREATIVITY

Using the intuition cards should never be a struggle. Let them become an opportunity that opens the door to a more relaxed and contemplative state of mind. Look forward to using them and enjoy the results. You will now use the cards to inspire creative thinking and will enjoy a fascinating experiment with the imagination. This experiment can be done at any time but is particularly useful to anyone engaged in a creative occupation. If you work on a computer, and need to take regular short five-minute breaks, the cards are an excellent way to use this otherwise wasted time.

EXPERIMENT IN CREATIVITY

The experiments you have done so far have identified images in the cards and then interpreted them as symbols arising from the subconscious. This next experiment is less targeted and should be used purely as a means to stimulate a creative flow of thought. In effect it is a form of daydreaming but with a serious purpose.

STEP 1. Prepare yourself

As you did in the first experiments, close your eyes

and relax. Let your mind float in that wonderful state between sleeping and wakefulness. Your mind is fluid yet you are fully alert. There is no need to set a specific problem to be solved. The objective of this exercise is to get you into a more creative state of mind, better to perform whatever task you have set yourself. This could be an idea for a new project, the plan for a new painting, developing a character for a novel etc. Once you achieve the right mental condition the ideas will come far more easily.

STEP 2. *Select a card*

Randomly choose a card from the pack or choose one that you feel drawn to. Look into the card and see how the pictures arise. As before, look into the white areas, into the details and remember to turn the card around to see what other pictures are formed. Don't worry about remembering the images that occur. In this instance you are not going to interpret them.

STEP 3. Encourage Fantasy

As the images arise, let your mind make up a fantasy about what you see. Let an imaginary play unfold. For example, if you see a strange face, make up a story about the person. Why do they look the way they do? What sort of person are they and what are their hopes, fears and ambitions? As well as the characters let the landscapes appear as well. Set the characters in the landscape and imagine the situations that unfold as one character interacts with another in these surreal environments. At first you will need deliberately to make up stories but, once the imagination is activated, strange tales will unfold naturally.

STEP 4. Apply yourself to your given task

By exercising the imagination in this way it frees you from the restraints of conventional thinking. By the time you've finished your head will be filled with all sorts of strange ideas. When you now apply yourself to your set project, ideas will come more naturally. The cards may have suggested some ideas already and you are now in the right state of mind to achieve the desired creative results. You are now thinking in a completely new way.

Using Intuition and Psychic Skills in Daily Life

The objective of this system is not only to use your intuition when you are working with the cards but also to allow your intuitive powers to influence every aspect of your life. You can listen to your intuition all the time. If you can learn to **trust** your intuition and **follow** your gut feeling about a situation you are taking the first step towards using ESP in everyday situations. So, if you feel you have a gift why not start using it?

Here's a few simple ways you can apply your skills:

LETTERS: You've applied for a new job and receive a hand written letter. Close your eyes as you hold the letter and observe what pictures pop into your head. What feelings do you get about the sender? Are they happy? What is the letter about? Look at the cards and see what pictures are shown to you. Psychics call this technique *psychometry* and you may find that your clairvoyant impressions may well prove correct. The cards can give you part of the answer but here you are extending the scope of your intuitive powers.

RELATIONSHIPS: ESP works best if you like the

people you're working with. And if you *love* them the powers become even more enhanced. You will know that your partner loves you as much as you love them if you find yourself finishing each other's sentences or have exactly the same thoughts. Try comparing your dreams—you may have exactly the same dreams and be resolving problems together. You may also tend to see similar images in the cards. Using the cards increases your awareness of ESP between you and the people who are important to you. They help you to trust your feelings

HEALTH: Psychic powers can be used to heal sick or troubled people. If you see something in the cards about someone's health, use your time immediately after the session to send healing thoughts. You are already linked to their vibration so it is easy now to extend this and to send them healing light. Imagine that they are well and happy. Then send them your telepathically transmitted healing thoughts. Imagine this as a healing ray of light that bathes the target person. It washes away their illness or problem and replaces it with powerful living light. Wherever you send a thought of love, healing energy follows.

IMPRESSIONS: Clearly the cards attune you to

your intuition and ESP powers; you should look for ways to use them in everyday situations. Start by trusting your hunches. When you meet someone for the first time, notice your immediate reaction. Do you like them? Remember your first impressions and test to see if they are proved in reality. Use you intuition to guess lottery numbers, the number of sweets in a bag, or the name of the next person to telephone you. With regular practice your intuitive ESP will increase.

DIRECTIONS: Learn to trust your sense of direction. Put away the map and trust your intuition. You'll be surprised to discover that your intuition will take you to your destination with uncanny accuracy. At first you'll make many mistakes but, with practice, you'll soon be able to find even the most obscure places without any knowledge of the area.

USING THE CARDS FOR ESP

Psychic powers are a natural gift that is latent in everybody. In prehistoric times telepathy would have been a useful ability to have as it could be used to give warnings of danger. In the times before language it could also have helped with the business of bonding or communication of ideas.

Clairvoyant abilities to 'remote view' distant locations would help in finding a new source of food or water. The ability to dowse may be a hand-me-down from these times. Furthermore, precognition—the ability to see the future—would have a survival function. Nature gave us psychic skills to help us survive and evolve. We are now going to use the cards to put us in touch with these forgotten powers.

THE CARDS AND PSYCHIC POWERS

When your imagination creates pictures in the cards, you are getting in touch with the hidden part of yourself—the subconscious mind. Here can be found access to the dormant psychic powers that humankind had in prehistoric times. The cards reveal your own inner-self but also within the images are reflections of information that is coming to you by paranormal means. As you read earlier, these techniques have been used for thousands of years in the many oracles that use random shapes and events as their basis.

Many of the images you see arise because of clairvoyance. They are not just about yourself but about your future. Many psychic techniques work simply by commanding the subconscious to give you an answer and then trusting the information you are given. Usually the first thought that comes to you is the right one. The skill is in sorting out which thoughts are your own and which have been given to you by your paranormal abilities.

THE CARDS AS AN ORACLE

Random oracles were once used as a means to tell the future. The pictures seen in the sacrificial fires, the entrails of animals or the patterns in sand could all reveal insights into what the fates hold for us. The first shaman priests must have relied entirely upon their own psychic intuition to determine what each individual image means. Indeed this is by far the best way to work as it directly involves the psychic powers.

However, as the oracles developed traditional meanings were given to specific images. Many of these meanings are still used in tea leaf reading and other oracles. Inevitably, various authors have given different interpretations to each picture and now many of the original meanings have been lost. From page 80 onwards we have provided a dictionary of symbols. You will already have worked with the psychological meanings but now you can begin working with the mystical meanings of the images seen. However, please use these only as a guide. It is your own inner hunches and gut feelings that will give you the most accurate insights. Trust these intuitive feelings.

VISIONS OF THE FUTURE

Forecasting the future is always a risky business. Sometimes a psychic can get it right with uncanny accuracy but at other times they can make big mistakes. Often, later, it is realized that the information received was correct but the interpretation of its meaning was wrong. For example, ancient Greek stories tell how king Croesus of Lydia asked the Delphi Oracle about the impending war with Persia. He was told "If you cross the river Halys a great nation will fall". The king went to war and crossed the river with confidence but his army was slaughtered in battle. A great nation did fall—but it was his own!

PERSONAL ORACLE EXPERIMENT

Clearly, it is important, when using any divination technique, to remember that it is easy to misinterpret what we 'see'. It is better to consider our insights as potentials and opportunities rather than unalterable fate. The objective of this next experiment is to gain insight into your *potential* future. Regard the information you receive as being like a map that will help you avoid the pitfalls and lead you to the best possible outcome.

STEP 1. Relax and get yourself into the right frame of mind as you have done in previous experiments.

STEP 2. Set yourself a target by thinking about an issue that you would like to address. Keep your question fairly open. The cards will not be able to give you yes and no answers. You are going to let them give you suggestions for future scenarios and solutions to problems.

STEP 3. Select a card at random and look at it to see what pictures unfold. Once again remember to look at both the black and white shapes as well as the small details. Allow images and pictures to unfold and involve yourself in whatever fantasies come to mind. As you did with the creative experiments, let mini plays unfold. Are you seeing potential outcomes for the future?

STEP 4. You may see happy or sad scenes. Remember that these are all potential events. Try to dig deeper and ask your own inner voice to guide you. What should you do to get the best result from your current circumstance? Be silent within for a few moments and answers will come to you. Your psychic intuition is trying to help you.

STEP 5. Inevitably, certain images will arise from the cards that you keep being drawn to. Once you have decided which are the most important ones, you can look these up in the mystical symbol meanings sections towards the back of this book.

STEP 6. When you have come to your conclusions about what the potential future holds, write down a simple message to yourself that gives you the most positive approach to take. Carry this affirmation with you to remind you about how your intuition has advised you to act. For example, you saw angry faces in the cards. This may indicate the root cause of the next problem you will face. So give yourself something to arm yourself in the period ahead. In this instance your affirmation may be "I shall conquer anger through love".

USING THE CARDS WITH OTHERS

Soon you are going to learn how to use your Inkblot Intuition Cards to give a reading for somebody else. However, before you do this, it is important that you consider your motives and decide how you can use the cards to help people.

Unfortunately there are many fortune tellers working today who do a great deal of harm and cause much unnecessary heartache by their lack of a basic code of conduct.

Remember that many of the things you see will be symbols. For example, if you see macabre images don't immediately assume that this is a prediction of a death. A genuine psychic knows that it is not possible to predict death—this is information that is denied us. Similarly, don't tell a person to go against their doctor's advice or you'll not only be in trouble with the law but may put someone at risk. Also, don't let your ego get in the way—the more you show off and boast, the more your psychic skills shrink away. Be confident, of course, and you can joke about how good you are, but don't take your ego too seriously.

It is also a mistake to make exaggerated claims. You are just starting to develop your skills so make certain that your sitter understands this. You can't guarantee to solve their problems. Try to be as clear as possible and let it flow. When your stream of psychic impressions stops, say so, and finish the reading. It's no good just making things up to fill in the time when nothing comes. It is better to give just a little good quality clairvoyance than lots of rubbish.

It is also important to get the sitter into a good mood when you work. Their energy is as important as your own for a successful session. Instill optimism and try to see beyond bad events to better times. Help them to overcome obstacles and stress how they have free will to make the future what they want it to be. Together you will find ways to encourage good fortune.

Strive to dig deeper with your clairvoyance. Discipline yourself never to be satisfied with what you give. If you get something correct, try adding more and being even more specific. A really good tip when you're stuck is to make your sitter laugh. Humor is an absolutely indispensable aid to good clairvoyance. Once a person smiles or laughs the barriers come down and the clairvoyant energy flows between you.

USING THE CARDS TO GIVE A PSYCHIC CONSULTATION

The Intuition Cards you have made predict the future by interpreting a random event. Carl Jung, the father of analytical psychology, called the laws that govern this process *synchronicity*. "Anything done at a particular moment in time has the qualities of that moment in time," he said. His theory, in simple terms, proposed that psychological events run in parallel to material ones. Hence, the powerful subconscious psyche attracts unusual coincidences. The Intuition cards are a focal point for these forces.

When you give a reading for another person, your own subconscious mind is acting as a channel for your psychic powers. For example, you receive a telepathic thought from the person and it is expressed in one of the images you see in the cards. Their mood may reflect the nature of what you see. If they feel depressed you may, in turn, notice depressing images in the cards.

In the main it is best to keep your sessions as light as possible and particularly when you first start using the cards. However, as you become more skilled, you will discover that this is an extremely powerful psychic tool.

THE ONE CARD READING

STEP 1. Chat with your sitter for a little while and help them relax. If they start telling you about the nature of their problem ask them not to. It's your job to tell them these things. The less you know about them the better your clairvoyance will be. There should be no preconceptions in your mind when you look at the cards. This isn't guesswork.

STEP 2. You can give a general reading or the sitter may prefer you to focus on a particular issue. If they request that you to ask the cards a question keep it simple. For example "Tell me if my son will marry Jenny or Sally who he left three times" would be better put as "tell me about my son". The second question doesn't give too much away.

STEP 3. Ask the sitter to take a card and hand it to you. Watch the pictures unfold as you would if you were using the cards for yourself. As usual, relax and let your mind flow. Watch for the shapes that appear in both the black and white areas.

STEP 4. As the pictures appear you will need to interpret these as images about the sitter's predicament. For example, you see a house. Listen to what your gut feeling is telling you and make your interpretation. "I feel that you are thinking about a move" or your interpretation could be something completely different such as "I feel that you are searching for domestic security." Your intuition will automatically know what each image means.

STEP 5. The images you see will reveal all about the person's current psychological state and life situation. Further images will reveal what they should and shouldn't do about them. Your intuitive powers may also contain predictions for the potential future.

CARDS FOR PAST PRESENT AND FUTURE

In this next section you are going to develop the one card reading and now use a simple spread. This will enable you to give a more detailed reading and will help you to identify which images refer to the past, present and future. This method will help you to target your psychic intuition.

STEP 1. Chat with your sitter for a little while and help them relax. When you both feel ready, ask them to take three cards from the pack. They can select any cards they feel drawn to or chose them at random. You can decide whether you let them choose the cards face up or down.

STEP 2. Ask them if they want a general reading or to address a specific question. Again keep it fairly open so that you are not unduly influenced by the innuendo in the question.

STEP 3. Lay the cards on the table in the way

indicated on the page opposite. Unlike tarot cards there is, of course, no upright and reversed meaning to these cards as they are symmetrical.

STEP 4. Pick up the card from the 'past conditions' and examine it. The images that come to you will relate to the past influences that created the present conditions. Your psychic intuition may also give you information about the sitter's distant past and even their childhood. If your psychic intuition gives you this information, tell your sitter about it, even if it's not relevant to the immediate issues you are dealing with. It is important to give the sitter information that they can qualify. If you can describe their past and present situation correctly then you are more likely to get their future right.

STEP 5. Now pick up the card from the 'present conditions' position. Your sitter may be keen to know the future but spend some time with this card so that your psychic intuition can fully involve itself in the issues that need to be addressed. Just hearing someone talk about and recognize their dilemma can be very therapeutic for the sitter. Again you will need to interpret the pictures you see as symbols of the sitter's experiences.

STEP 6. Finally pick up the 'future conditions' card.

If your psychic intuition has correctly described the past and present you can feel confident that what you see for the future will also be correct. Remember, of course, that you are being given symbols and each one needs to be interpreted. Make sure you do this with sympathy for their suffering and offer kind words and timely succor. You are here to help them—not frighten them.

THREE CARD SPREAD

CARD 1 PAST CONDITIONS: This card represents the influences that are passing away or have caused the situation.

CARD 2 PRESENT CONDITIONS: This card represents the enquirer's present circumstances and the nature of the problems confronting them.

CARD 3 FUTURE CONDITIONS: This card refers to the potential outcome and trends. Your advice may help them avoid pitfalls and move towards good fortune.

DESIGNING YOUR OWN SPREADS

The intuition cards you have made are a flexible system of oracle that can be adapted and changed according to your own needs and preferences. Many clairvoyants now use the cards in conjunction with other systems such as the tarot. For example, a reader may use one of the intuition cards to give a preliminary intuitive reading in order to help them link with the client. They can also be useful as a means to help the psychic intuition throw light on a tarot card that seems incongruous with the rest of the cards in the spread.

The Intuition Cards are also ideal to use with the Chinese oracle called the *I Ching*. It is good to contemplate the cards while thinking about the words of wisdom given you by this oracle. In this way your subconscious mind is given a means to focus its attention and help you interpret the hidden meaning of the words through pictures.

As well as using the cards in conjunction with other systems, you can devise spreads of your own that suit you or can be used for specific questions. So long as you decide upon a spread and keep to it, the laws of synchronicity will ensure that the randomly drawn cards correspond with the conditions marked by the card positions.

On the next pages are a few examples of spreads you can try.

FIVE CARD HORSE SHOE SPREAD

This spread can be used to give a more detailed view of the future

CARD 1: The past conditions

CARD 2: Hidden influences that have a bearing upon the present conditions.

CARD 3: The present situation

CARD 4: The near future

CARD 5: The distant future

THE ONE YEAR SPREAD

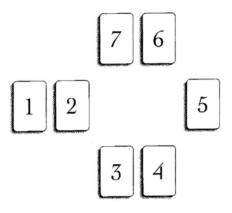

This spread can be used to predict for the year ahead. You will start your interpretation from the current month.

CARD 1: The current circumstances

Interpret this card first as you did in the one card experiment but without the use of prediction. The cards for the months can be read one at a time in sequence to build a picture of the year ahead.

CARD2: The situation in January and February

CARD 3: The situation in March and April

CARD 4: The situation in May and June

CARD 5: The situation in July August

CARD 6: The situation in September and October

CARD 7: The situation in November and December

THE RELATIONSHIP SPREAD

In this spread the three cards on the left represent the sitter and the three on the right represent the sitter's current partner.

CARD 1: The sitter. Interpret this card to describe how the sitter feels about their current relationship.

CARD 2: The partner. The images arising from this card describes how the sitter's partner feels about them.

CARD 3: The sitter's environment: this card describes the influences around the sitter

CARD 4: The partner's environment: this card describes the influences around the partner.

CARD 5: The outcome. The images seen in the last card hint at possible solutions to resolve problems or plan a reconciliation or parting of the ways. Again remember to advise your sitter that this is intuitive guidance and not necessarily prediction.

THE VOICES OF ANGELS

The Intuition cards put you in touch with your own inner voice. In themselves they do nothing. You are making and using the cards as a way to get in touch with the very powerful psychological and spiritual forces that we call called the intuition. Since earliest times, wise people have been guided by their inner voice. Sometimes the inner wisdom comes through dreams and at other times it appears as the divine voice from the angels or God and has inspired prophets and saints. Today most people have lost touch with their inner voice and feel to be at the mercy of their troubles.

How to Develop the Inner Voice

It is, of course, open to debate whether the inner voice is just the subconscious processes at work or is indeed inspired by supernatural powers. Certainly it appears that the powers of ESP can unfold by listening to the still, small voice within. For some people the inner 'voice' speaks with words but for others the language from within comes as pictures or sensations.

Many mystical traditions, such as anthroposophy and some forms of Buddhism believe that the inner voice is the divine 'overself' communicating to us. It is the part of ourselves that has never been born and lives outside of time and space as we understand it. This overself is all-knowing and understands the reasons why we suffer and the purpose of our life on earth. Sometimes it interrupts our routines to give spiritual guidance. By listening to it we draw close to our spiritual heart and away from the base desires and pettiness of the lower self.

Other traditions, such as Spiritualism, Spiritism and Theosophy claim that the inner voice comes from spiritual beings who live on a higher dimension of existence. We may think of them as the spirit guides or the angels. Spiritualist mediums, of course, believe that these discarnate beings can influence our thoughts and give us direct guidance about what to do in our lives. All we have to do is to still the mind, during meditation or quiet reflection, and the spirit beings will draw close to share their wisdom with us.

The highest of all the intuitive voices is the conscience. Every one of us has a sense of what is right and wrong and this knowledge seems to be something that has not been learnt from experience. It is a perennial knowledge that arises in every generation. It is the innate knowledge of what is right.

Some say that the conscience is the voice of God that transcends all cultural barriers and creeds. It is the source of the universal knowledge and has unlimited wisdom. Everyone has it. It is what Hindus call the heart. All we have to do is be humble enough to listen to its inner prompting and we will do the right thing in every situation and grow to become better people. The inkblot intuition cards are your way to harmonize with this wonderful inner power.

Internalizing Clairvoyance

So far you have been mainly working with the inkblot cards and using them as a sounding board for your inner process. Your next step is to internalize this process and begin to see the symbolic images in your mind's eye. By doing this you will telepathically 'pick up' information about the person you are reading and will have no need of any cards, tools or props in the future. You will inwardly 'see' images and pictures while you are sitting with them and will describe and interpret the symbols you 'see'. We are now moving towards the advanced stages of clairvoyance and mediumship that I describe in my other book called *Psychic School* (Available from my website at psychics.co.uk or directly from Amazon)

Internal Images

When starting out as a psychic you will find that your dreams naturally become very vivid as your inner world adapts to the newfound psychic abilities that you are deliberately encouraging to flower. Dreams are also a powerful way to activate and develop your psychic abilities. You know how to read images that you see in random shapes; now I want you to become aware of the internal imagery that is continually being generated in your subconscious mind. When we sleep, our dreams are a constant flow of images and symbols that write themselves into metaphors and allegories about our lives, thoughts and emotions and, within these strange images, psychic insights are entwined.

Sometimes, just as you fall asleep, you may experience an incredible flow of incredible imagery that seems to appear fully formed out of nowhere. These are called hypnagogic dreams and happen to some people at the point between waking and sleep. No formal study has been made but, from my own anecdotal evidence, it would seem that most of the psychic and mediumistic people I meet experience this state regularly. As well as amazing imagery, people will sometimes see phosphenes—brilliant patterns of light—which can manifest as intricate mandalas and random speckles. There may be feelings of visually moving through tunnels of light. The images are fleeting and given to very rapid changes. These images and symbols are not like normal dreams but are extremely vivid and have no narrative.

As part of your spiritual practice I suggest that you encourage hypnagogic dreams as it will help you to connect with the imagery that is flowing in the background of your awareness when you give readings. By learning to connect with the messages that spontaneously arise from the subconscious mind, you will soon learn also to receive information that comes to you through clairvoyance. What happens with clairvoyance is that information just drops into your awareness and you haven't the faintest idea where it came from. All these techniques that I and other psychic mediums teach, ultimately bring you to this point:

you simply trust what you get. You then simply relay the information that comes to you to the person you are giving the reading to and—with luck—they will be able to verify it as correct. The same happens with mediumship: a name, for example, will drop into your awareness from out of the blue and you simply repeat it. "Do you know someone called Frederick Coopers?" They looked stunned: "Yes how did you know that?" There is no way of explaining that the message came from spirit but somehow I just knew the name and how it relates to them.

By encouraging hypnagogic dreaming you open yourself to the possibility of information entering your awareness that has not been censored by your rational mind, which tends to block the free-flow of clairvoyance. If you have ever experienced this strange state of awareness, you will know that the visions, which are seen, are remarkable and may include vivid pictures and scenes that are astonishing in their clarity.

Some people use hypnagogic dreaming as a means to trigger out of body travel, and retrocognition (visions of the past and sometimes past-lives) and it can also be used to induce lucid dreams (waking up in a dream as it is taking place). Although the images in a hypnagogic dream are very hard to recall afterwards, I have also sometimes used this state to look into the future. If the stream of awareness is targeted to a specific subject—such as what will tomorrow's newspaper headline be—I have found that these dreams often reveal images relating to the future.

Tips to Open Your Psychic Powers

You are probably a lot more psychic than you think. Start by trying these simple tips to discover your latent abilities:

BELIEVE IN YOURSELF. Parapsychologists have found that people who believe in psychic powers often score better in tests than sceptics. So start trusting your gut feelings, for this is the voice of your intuition that links you to your sixth sense.

BECOME AWARE. Look for examples of psychic phenomena in everyday life. For example you may be able to anticipate what is going to happen. Tune in to people's emotions and try to anticipate their mood. Also, keep a note of the odd things that happen to you, in order to increase your awareness of your powers.

ENJOY BEING PSYCHIC. Are you bright and

bubbly? ESP experiments have concluded that outgoing, extrovert personalities score better in tests than somber, reflective types.

BE CREATIVE. Artistic activities, such as painting or sketching things that are on your mind, can often allow the intuition to express itself. A large proportion of psychics come from an artistic background. Some researchers believe that this is because psychics, like artists, predominantly use the right-hand side of their brain—the side that's responsible for intuition.

RECORD YOUR DREAMS. If you teach yourself to remember your dreams you will become more in tune with the intuitive side of yourself. And it's from this part of you that your psychic powers arise. The simplest method of dream recall is to keep a dream diary and write down your dreams every morning. If you cannot remember a dream, just write down whatever is on your mind. We dream every single night and eventually you will fill your dream diary with lots of dreams. As well as being an interesting insight into your hidden self, they may occasionally reveal glimpses of the future.

TRUST YOUR INTUITION. That gut feeling may

be right. Much of the information we get through intuition is gained clairvoyantly. Women trust their intuition more than men: 85 per cent of people who report paranormal events are women.

You will improve your psychic powers as you interact with people and experience unfamiliar places. Here's a few simple ways to enhance your abilities:

LOVERS. If you have ever been deeply in love, you are likely to have experienced telepathy—the psychic ability to read minds. Lovers send subtle signals to each other. 'He/She knows just what I'm thinking' is a common statement in the early stages of love—and we attribute it to being in love instead of accepting it as part of an innate psychic ability. You can improve your psychic awareness by paying attention to these signals.

Love test: Try to guess what your loved one is about to say, or finish sentences for him/her. Sharing thoughts may come naturally to you. Compare dreams to see if any of them are the same.

CHILDREN. If you're a new mother, you'll almost certainly have experienced the sensation of knowing that your child is distressed when you're not in the room or sensing when he's about to wake up for a feed. In fact, experiments have shown that if a newborn child is put into a soundproof room, mothers still know exactly when the child is distressed, even though they can't see or hear their child. For example it has been found that the mother's heart beat increases slightly as soon as the child wakes or becomes distressed.

Kid test: Practicing your psychic skills with children can be fun. Try guessing which advertisement is going to be next on the TV or, when driving, what color car is going to come along the road next. Perhaps you could try describing a place that you've never been to and, when you get there, see who comes closest to the truth.

STRANGERS. Experiments have also shown that many people can tell when they are being stared at. The heartbeat increases slightly. This is another example of how psychic powers may be a dormant survival skill. In the jungle, it would have been very useful to know if an animal is starring at us or stalking us from the undergrowth. You can try it for yourself.

Stranger test: In a public place try staring at a stranger who has their back to you. You will be surprised how often they show signs of discomfort or turn around and look at you. It is showing how you are using the psychic power of telepathy to influence another person.

PLACES. The thought vibrations that people give off are absorbed into the environment. A psychically sensitive person can feel these vibrations, which we commonly refer to as the *atmosphere* of a place. For example, you may notice that a church has a very special spiritual atmosphere. This is partly created by the architecture of the building, the smells and the colored lights of the stained glass. However, there is also 'something else': you can 'feel' the years of worship in the very fabric of the building. Like a sponge, the church has absorbed the vibrations of all the people that have worshiped there. Similarly, some places have a bad atmosphere. Imagine what horrible vibrations you would sense in an abattoir or the death camps at Belsen.

Place test: Become aware of the atmosphere of the places you visit. If you are invited to visit a person's home for the first time, sense whether it is a happy place or not. If it is a comparatively new purchase try sensing who lived there before. Maybe the new owner will be able to confirm your feelings. You can greatly enhance your psychic skills by sensitizing yourself to the atmosphere of places.

Something Fun to Try:

One psychic projection technique that I like to practice is to sit on a bench in a shopping center and stare hard at people who are walking away from me. You can attract their attention by telepathy and they will often stop in their tracks and turn around to look. Scientists have researched this and have found that people's heart rate increases when they are being secretly stared at. Telepathy works best if it is charged with emotion. When connecting, try to project feelings of alarm or danger and the targeted person is more likely to turn and look at you.

You can also try planting a thought in a person's mind. For example I carried a picture of an apple with the words from W B Yates written below it saying "The Silver Apples of the Moon, The Golden Apples of the Sun". I would then think about this while people were talking to me or a group of people were talking. It is amazing how many people mentioned, silver, gold, apples, the moon or, in one instance, the poet Yates. I would then shock them by explaining what I had done and would show them the picture of the apple with the verse from the poem. Make cards with words and pictures of your own to try similar thought projection experiments

Training Your Psychic Gifts

The best way to train any skill is to practice it. Once you have the courage to try out your psychic skills with an open-minded friend, you are likely to see them improve tremendously. I have trained a great may psychics and mediums and the best method I have found to get people started is to practice a skill known as psychometry. This will tell you things about the person's present and past life. It is not a method of foretelling the future.

In this next psychic experiment you will again work with imagery and symbols but this time will interpret them as they arise directly from your subconscious. So for example if in your mind's eye you see a flying bird this may be taken as literal— they may keep birds for example—or it may be symbolic: the bird may represent their desire for freedom and so on. Up to this point you have been working with images and something in front of you. Now, apart from holding onto an object, you have to rely on what is coming directly to you from your own intuition. The key is to remind yourself that you really do know the answers. Just let the knowledge come to you and you may startle yourself as to how much you can get right.

If you have been working with the inkblots and other techniques described so far, you will by now have become connected to the spiritual part of yourself that 'sees' images and symbols. Some refer to this as clairvoyance, which comes from the French *clair* meaning 'clear' and voir meaning 'to see'. When you do the next experiment you will also need to describe your feelings and impressions as well. The technique of psychometry that you will briefly learn now, helps a psychic person to describe the life and character of a person by holding an object that they have owned. We can only touch upon this here but I have described these techniques in detail in my other book, *Psychic School*, which continues and expands upon the basic teachings in this book.

HOW TO DO PSYCHOMETRY

Just as places pick up vibrations so too do objects worn by a person. By holding an object that belongs to the person, it's possible to glean all kinds of details about that person: for example if they have been through pain or suffering, or how many children they have.

Now try psychometry for yourself.

STEP 1. Ask a friend if you can hold something personal that belongs to someone they know well. The history of the object should be known to your friend but not to you. You are now going to try to describe the life and character of the owner.

STEP 2. Relax and let your thoughts flow. Now say exactly what comes to mind. Do not censor your thoughts. However silly it may sound, say exactly what pops into your head.

STEP 3. Imagine that the person who owns the object is standing right in front of you. Are they a warm person or a cold person? Are they happy or sad? Perhaps they are a worrier. What are they good at doing? What sort of skills do they have? Can you trust this person? What are their good points? And—be careful with this one—what are their bad points?

STEP 4. Once you have described the character, try intuitively to perceive a few specific facts about the person. What was their childhood like? What does their home look like? What sort of people do they mix with? Can you see any specific events that may have changed the course of their life?

STEP 5. When you feel you have finished, ask your friend to tell you what percentage you got right. You may really surprise yourself with your accuracy. Don't be disheartened if you are off track at first. And don't forget to check the facts with the owner of the object. There may be all sorts of things that you discover, which they may never have told anyone about.

Psychometry is a way to teach a fledgling psychic or medium to describe the personality and life of a person who has owned an object. Although images and symbols received from the intuition can give a lot of psychic information, the ability to describe a person's character and their hidden thoughts, hopes and fears is a critical part of giving a reading. You have learnt a lot so far about attuning to your own intuition and listening to its messages. When you engage in the deeper forms of psychic work you will find that you can also access the subconscious mind of the person consulting you. You will 'see' their thoughts in your mind's eye and notice you may be reflecting their feelings. When giving a reading you need to be very attentive of everything that is passing through your awareness, for the impressions that you are getting are not your own but arising from the person sitting with you.

Thoughts and feelings that are alien to your normal mental state may be coming from them so, for example, if you have a feeling of being angry and determined, you may ask them: "Would I be right in saying that you are sometimes quite an angry person but this anger fuels your tremendous determination?" This is just an example, of course, but note all the many different thoughts and feelings you experience while reading and express them as you give the consultation. You will also pick up memories that are not yours as well as the person's hopes, disappointments and fears.

All of the above takes many years of practice and it can take a long time to recognize which thoughts are your own and which ones are being received intuitively from the people you are reading. And, of course, you have to test your abilities with others so that they can verify that you can give credible information, which they can verify.

I am now moving beyond the remit of this book, which has been to show the absolute beginner how to get started with psychic work. The inkblot method is a good starting point but if you want to progress further you will need to learn many more techniques such as meditation, spirit attunement, opening the chakras, aura sensing and so on. The work you have done so far is a good start and you are, I hope, a little more prepared to continue your journey of psychic discovery.

PART 3

DICTIONARY OF SYMBOLS

Every image that comes up in the Intuition Cards means something, but the same image may mean different things to different people and different things to you at different times in your life. It would be impossible to list all the possible images you may see in the Intuition Cards. The purpose of this next section is therefore to present a selection of *possible* meanings to help you form your own judgements. It is up to you to select the interpretation that seems to apply to your particular situation. Please do not be too literal with the following examples. In the end it's *your* interpretation that counts.

Interpreting the cards is not the difficult task that it may seem at first. It is something you will soon master and enjoy doing. You must have a respectful attitude towards the cards and a belief that they have something valuable to say as well as a determination to be open and honest with yourself. In many instances, you will discover that the people, faces, places, objects and events you see in the cards represent parts of yourself. They symbolize your feelings, fears, desires, attitudes and so on. There are many aspects of your personality that you do not know about or have not acknowledged. The *Intuition Cards* will teach you to be honest with yourself.

Every entry in the symbol dictionary has two sections: the Psychological Meaning and the Mystical Meaning:

THE PSYCHOLOGICAL MEANING

These sections tell you what the symbolism of the cards says about you and your psychology. The images you see reflect your deepest emotional responses to your waking-life experiences. A correct interpretation of the card's symbolism will only be possible if they are viewed in the context of your outward life. This will include your current situation and your current problems, fears, hopes ambitions and so on. The cards may also refer to your past and to your attitudes that are deeply seated or brought forward from your childhood. You may also find that they reflect your hates, prejudices, fears, guilt feelings and habits.

By becoming aware of these qualities within yourself you will get to know yourself better and enable the subconscious co-operate with you. You will start to take control of your life and begin to determine your own future.

It is also worth remembering that not every image you see has a profound meaning and psychological significance. Some of the pictures you see may be reflecting your everyday thoughts. Some may just be a repetition of the day's events. Sometimes the things you see reflect what you've seen on the TV, read in a book or been thinking about. Not every image you see will contain a life-transforming revelation. Some images will be trivial but others will be serious and significant.

THE MYSTICAL MEANING

The mystical meanings of the images are taken from the traditional superstitions and meanings found in tealeaf reading, pyromancy, scrying and other systems of divination. They are traditional omens and predictions for the future. Again you must make your own interpretation for the true prophetic meaning of each symbol. Don't get too serious or literal. Have fun with these but, when it comes to true clairvoyance, you will need to turn to your own inner powers of prophecy

PEOPLE, FACES AND PARTS OF THE BODY

Faces:

Psychological meaning: Faces are some of the most likely images you will see in the cards. Often they will appear distorted but consider the expression. Does it say something about your state of mind? You may have feelings of repressed anger, resentment or you may harbor hidden fears. Also the face may remind you of someone you know. What does this person represent about your own personality?

Angry Face: This may represent your own anger or the anger of someone around you.

Happy Face: Faces express emotions. Have you found happiness or is this your goal?

Sad Face: A predominance of sad faces may indicate that you are more depressed about an issue than you care to admit.

Weird Face: Don't be worried by strange faces—you're not about to go mad. Faces can be made out of all sorts of shapes. Think about how the emotions expressed by the face make you feel. Your emotional response may reveal the answer to your question.

Lover's Face: If the face reminds you of someone you know then consider what bearing this person has on the question you asked. They could represent an aspect of your own personality

Your Face: If the image reminds you of yourself you may be worried or concerned about your own self-image and how the world sees you. A face that reminds you of yourself can also show that you can understand yourself from another's point of view.

Confused Face: This may highlight your own inner confusion about what to do.

Frightening Face: Get behind the image and find out what it is that frightens you. Perhaps you are afraid to express your true feelings or feel insecure in some way.

Two Faces communicating: This may simply indicate the need to communicate your ideas to others or your desire to express what you are feeling.

Mystical Meaning: One face indicates a change but many indicate a party. Pleasant faces foretell happiness and prosperity but unpleasant ones indicate loss. To see a stranger's face means a change of residence.

Judge:

Psychological meaning: This could represent your conscience or worries about a conflict with authority.
Mystical Meaning: Setbacks and hardships.

Violent people:

Psychological Meaning: If the images you see are of a violent theme then there may be a need for you to express your emotions in a natural, gentle way.
Mystical Meaning: It is considered a good omen if you see violent images in the cards

Policeman:

Psychological Meaning: Are you feeling guilty about something?

Mystical Meaning: You have a secret enemy.

PEOPLE, FACES AND PARTS OF THE BODY CONTINUED

Queen:

Psychological Meaning: Shows the motherly side of your nature or the guiding intuitive self. Your intuition will guide your future.
Mystical Meaning: A helpful friend.

King:

Psychological Meaning: The king can show the masculine side of your nature. He can represent the intellect.
Mystical Meaning: A powerful ally.

Lovers:

Psychological Meaning: This symbol can have many meanings. On one level it can represent your thoughts about your personal relationships yet it can also signify the union of opposites within the psyche, such as the integration of reason and intuition. It shows inner harmony.
Mystical Meaning: Happiness and contentment.

Hands:

Psychological Meaning: Hands can represent dexterity and skill but are also a symbol of self-expression. Depending on the gesture they may be saying stop, hug me, goodbye or be beckoning you to something new.

Mystical Meaning: If the hand is outstretched, someone close to you needs held. If the hand is clenched, expect a surprise.

Heads:

Psychological Meaning: These may represent your behavior. A large head may represent intelligence or egotism. A square head may suggest a conformist and a shrunken head may suggest a feeling of inadequacy.

Mystical Meaning: Heads indicate new opportunities.

Teeth:

Psychological Meaning: According to the trance psychic, Edgar Cayce, teeth and tongues are a symbols for too much talking. Loose teeth may indicate careless talk whereas crooked teeth can indicate bad language or slander. Teeth falling out can indicate hidden anxieties.

Mystical Meaning: To see teeth or a tongue brings good luck.

Hair:

Psychological Meaning: Tangled hair can indicate a personal difficulty but straight hair shows that you are sorting a problem out.
Mystical Meaning: There is a whole fortune-telling system based around hair. Luxuriant long hair denotes continued health and prosperity. Frizzy or short curly hair indicates the opposite.

Ears:

Psychological Meaning: You may need to listen to what people are saying. You may be missing some very good advice.
Mystical Meaning: Unexpected news.

Eyes:

Psychological Meaning: Eyes represent the spiritual state of the individual and your perception of the world. It is the way you see things and how you interpret a situation.
Mystical Meaning: You will overcome difficulties if you take great care in all your dealings.

CREATURES

Spider:

Psychological Meaning: You may distrust others. Be careful about entering formal agreements—you may get trapped.

Mystical Meaning: This indicates a determined yet secretive person. Can also indicate money coming.

Birds:

Psychological Meaning: Birds are a symbol of transcendence. Consider the type of bird that you see. A dove may symbolize peace to come; a raven, deceit, and a peacock warns you to beware of pride. Butterflies may symbolize the spiritual transformation of the soul.

Mystical Meaning: Troubles between people will soon be over. Birds can also signify unexpected journeys.

Owl:

Psychological Meaning: You will gain greater wisdom.

Mystical Meaning: There will be gossip, scandal and failure.

Cat:

Psychological Meaning: Normally associated with female qualities, the cat may symbolize the female part of yourself—your intuition, maybe, or your psychic self. Associated with good fortune, it could also indicate a good period ahead.
Mystical Meaning: A false friend causes a quarrel.

Dog:

Psychological Meaning: A dog can be a symbol of devoted friendship. In myth it is often the guide—sometimes symbolizing the wisdom of the intuition. Violent dogs may show anger and your desire to express your hidden resentment.
Mystical Meaning: An emblem of faithfulness or envy. If it is at the top of the card it shows faithful friends but, if at the bottom, it shows extreme jealousy.

Fish:

Psychological Meaning: Fish are a universal symbol of fertility with the promise of personal inner growth. Superstitions say that to dream of catching a fish means good fortune will come your way.
Mystical Meaning: Fish denote successful events by water. Fate may call you to a distant place.

Horse:

Psychological Meaning: A horse can represent untamed emotions or even sexual ecstasy. Horseshoes, of course, are a well-known symbol of luck to come.

Mystical Meaning: If the horse is galloping this indicates good news from a lover. If you see only the head it means you will soon experience romance.

Pig:

Psychological Meaning: Are you being stubborn and "pig Headed"? It is also a symbol of selfishness and a brutish nature.

Mystical Meaning: You will have material success but also emotional problems.

Snakes:

Psychological Meaning: This can be a sexual symbol, a symbol of transformation or a symbol of healing.

Mystical Meaning: The emblem of falsehood and enmity. In some systems it can represent the triumph over an enemy.

Rats:

Psychological Meaning: Aspects of yourself or others

that probably frighten or disgust you. There could be problems ahead.

Mystical Meaning: Treachery is afoot.

Zoo Animals:

Psychological Meaning: You may feel that your life is hemmed in. You feel caged.

Mystical Meaning: An omen that you will be freed from your difficulties. In particular, a zebra indicates travel and an unsettled life.

Butterfly:

Psychological Meaning: A symbol of transcendence and rebirth. This positive symbol indicates that you are feeling inspired and fulfilled.

Mystical Meaning: You may fritter away your money in frivolous pursuits.

Crocodile:

Psychological Meaning: This could represent your hidden fears that lurk below the surface of your awareness.

Mystical Meaning: Beware of an enemy.

Lion:

Psychological Meaning: A lion may represent

confidence of pride. It can be a symbol of the self.
Mystical Meaning: Good luck with people of high rank. Be careful of people who may be envious of your success.

Elephant:

Psychological Meaning: This can be a symbol of inner strength and wisdom. It may also represent distant memories.
Mystical Meaning: A symbol of lasting success and the removal of obstacles.

Donkey:

Psychological Meaning: You may feel that you are overworked. Can also symbolize gentleness. A mule indicates stubbornness.
Mystical Meaning: You must be patient and optimistic.

Monkey:

Psychological Meaning: A trickster figure. It can represent the lower mind: the bad side of yourself that sometimes gets the better of you.
Mystical Meaning: Beware of a person who will flatter you.

Tortoise:

Psychological Meaning: This may represent the outer personality: the persona you hide behind.
Mystical Meaning: You will be unfairly criticized.

PLACES AND OBJECTS

Train:

Psychological Meaning: The direction of your life at the moment. Be careful that you don't miss an opportunity.
Mystical Meaning: One tree promises good health. Several trees denote that your wish will be accomplished. If they are accompanied by tiny blots or dots it indicates that your good fortune can be found at a distance.

Tree:

Psychological Meaning: Does the tree bear fruit? Is it strong like the oak or rotten, withered and battered. Trees are strong yet they can bend with the wind. Perhaps you should do the same when faced with adversity?
Mystical Meaning: A tree indicates changes for the better and ambitions fulfilled. If small inkblots or dots surround it, you will find your success in the

country.

Path:

Psychological Meaning: The direction you are taking in life. Note any other symbols you may see near this image.
Mystical Meaning: Shapes that suggest paths or roads indicate a journey.

Rose:

Psychological Meaning: A symbol of love and a mystical symbol for enlightenment. You may see other flowers in the inkblot. They can show the unfolding of something positive in your life or the development of your true potential.
Mystical Meaning: Ancient systems of fortune telling say that flowers, and particularly the rose, foretell great success in the arts and sciences. For married people it can also indicate healthy children.

Garden:

Psychological Meaning: A garden may represent inner peace and harmony.
Mystical Meaning: You have good and consistent friends.

House:

Psychological Meaning: A house can represent you or your body. Its state of repair indicates your physical or psychological health.
Mystical Meaning: To see a house foretells a period of contentment and security.

Windmill:

Psychological Meaning: This may be a symbol of work or of plenty. It may show how the wind of fortune drives your life.
Mystical Meaning: Success comes only through hard work.

Ladder:

Psychological Meaning: Progress in spiritual or worldly status.
Mystical Meaning: A happy union.

MORE PLACES AND OBJECTS

Revolver:

Psychological Meaning: Do you feel angry about something. Or perhaps you will get 'another shot' at an opportunity.
Mystical Meaning: Trouble and quarrels ahead.

Bridge: *Psychological Meaning:* A transition to new things. What do you see lying beyond? Is it a happy landscape or a forbidding one? You may have some good times or difficult decisions ahead. *Mystical Meaning:* An opportunity for success.

Moon:

Psychological Meaning: The moon has always been linked with fertility and may show personal growth. As the moon is associated with water, the inner growth may be emotional. There could be travel overseas predicted.
Mystical Meaning: The moon can represent a love affair, particularly if it is a new moon.

Mountains:

Psychological Meaning: A quest and obstacles to be overcome.
Mystical Meaning: This can represent obstacles or high ambitions.

Church:

Psychological Meaning: The sacred side of you will be of importance.
Mystical Meaning: A church can represent disappointment.

Door:

Psychological Meaning: The opening to a new area of your life. An opportunity ahead.
Mystical Meaning: A door can represent a strange occurrence.

Hat:

Psychological Meaning: Symbolizes your role in life. Perhaps a change of job or role is indicated.
Mystical Meaning: A hat can represent a new occupation.

Keys:

Psychological Meaning: A problem will be solved and you will be opening the door to opportunity.
Mystical Meaning: A key represents new opportunities.

Knife:

Psychological Meaning: Someone may mean you harm or you could have a self-destructive tendency.
Mystical Meaning: Lawsuits, broken relationships and divorce.

MYTH AND MAGIC

Angel:

Psychological Meaning: This could represent your desire to become more spiritual or to rise above the commonplace. As an omen for the future it augers well and peace may come to you. The angel of death may be a premonition of someone dying or an indication that your attitudes must go through a death and rebirth.

Mystical Meaning: A forecast of good news ahead.

Devil:

Psychological Meaning: A devil may represent the negative side of your own personality such as the qualities of envy, greed, lust, anger, hatred and so on. It may also represent the things you fear.

Mystical Meaning: Indicates evil influences and betrayal.

Fairy:

Psychological Meaning: A fairy may represent the undiscovered side of your own nature or be a reference to your childhood. You may wish for a little magic in your life.

Mystical Meaning: Most oracles consider fairies to be good omens.

Phoenix:

Psychological Meaning: A symbol of rebirth. You have been through some difficult times but now you feel a sense of renewed hope and optimism.
Mystical Meaning: A new start.

Dragon:

Psychological Meaning: An evil dragon may represent your hidden fears. It can represent the fears that block your way to the treasure of self-knowledge.
Mystical Meaning: In Chinese oracles the dragon is a symbol of the masculine power of yang and brings activity and creativity.

Wizard:

Psychological Meaning: A good wizard may represent the higher self within you. He is your innate knowledge that comes through intuition.
Mystical Meaning: You will experience many changes.

Witch:

Psychological Meaning: This figure may represent the shadow side of yourself. She symbolizes everything you have pushed out of your thoughts:

the bad feelings and thoughts that you refuse to recognize.

Mystical Meaning: Witches are an ill omen and indicate problems ahead.

Unicorn:

Psychological Meaning: Unicorns represent power, gentility and purity. They can be an expression of inspiration and wonder at the marvels of the inner world.

Mystical Meaning: You will have some correspondence in connection with official affairs.

Giant:

Psychological Meaning: Giants can represent awe-inspiring powers that are dominating you or forcing you to take notice of them. They are often associated with male sexuality.

Mystical Meaning: A lucky omen that predicts commercial success.

PART 4

BONUS CHAPTER: DEVELOPING MEDIUMSHIP

I am now going to give you a little taster of the advanced stages of spiritual development and explain a little about mediumship. This is the ability to communicate with the spirits of people who have passed into the next life. You cannot learn mediumship simply by reading books as it requires a person to sit in a development circle for many years for this gift to flower. However, what follows may help prepare you for your future spiritual work. I have described how to find or set up a psychic development circle in my book *Psychic School*, which takes you through the next stages of psychic and mediumistic development.

First Steps to Becoming a Medium

By now your psychic skills should have begun to develop. What follows is only an outline of the basics of mediumistic development but it should get you started. To fully develop these gifts, I advise you seek the guidance of a practicing medium and preferably a medium who has worked or is working within Spiritualism.

THE CASE FOR LIFE-AFTER-DEATH

Belief in an afterlife goes back to the beginnings of human history. It is not a new phenomenon. In this age of materialism, however, belief is not enough and demands are now made to prove survival.

Some of you reading this may already have had this proof through mediumship, as did many great names throughout history including: Sir Arthur Conan Doyle, William Crooks, Madam Curie, Lord Downing, Thomas Edison, Queen Victoria to name just a few. Those who claim that mediumship is purely fraud must consider how so many great and inquiring minds could have been duped.

Some of the most important studies of spirit communication by mediums has been extensively carried out by the Society of Psychical Research. When one of its founders, F W Myers, died a group of unconnected mediums—one living in England, another in America and a third in India—started to receive messages from Myers. The resulting transcripts became known as the Cross-Correspondences. Myers communicated a fragmented series of messages that only made sense when all three mediums' evidence could be collected together. As if to give further proof, Myers made references, in his communications, to obscure ancient Greek texts that were far beyond the knowledge or education of the mediums involved.

SPIRIT EVIDENCE FOR SURVIVAL

In my own work I am sometimes perplexed by the intricate proof that a spirit communicator can transmit. For example I recall a communication I made at a Spiritualist Church. I was able to give the communicators first and second name and explained that he had been singing *Rule Britannia* as he died. Also I said that he died in Londonderry, was to marry in two weeks and that his fiancé was to have a baby. The man had died in Londonderry and saved his friends from the blast by throwing himself onto a terrorist bomb. As he did so he sang rule Britannia.

On another occasion, and there are many I could quote, I described for one sitter her sister in spirit who had died in a road accident. I saw her buried in her wedding dress, clutching a china doll that held a blue rose. I saw a letter and was able to quote its words exactly.

My wife Jane, who is also a medium, has not only helped the living to contact the dead, but has been requested on many occasions to help people who are in the process of dying. When our friend, Keith Moore, lay dying from cancer of the spleen, his last request was that Jane should be with him. His mother, a Spiritualist, agreed and called Jane to his deathbed. Jane was able to ease the passing considerably. She helped him link up with the spirit friends that had come for Keith—spirit people stood in the room whom Keith could also see for himself.

Jane, too, has accurately read notes left in the coffins. For a severely bereaved couple she was able to describe their son and say that he was buried in his yellow football shirt. She gave the child's full name, his date of passing, the message his mother had given him and even the number printed on the shirt. Everyone in the room was astonished when they heard the young boy call out in a real voice "Mum".

How can this type of evidence ever be considered as self-deception or the reading of facial clues? We'd never met most of these people before in our life.

Many ordinary people, who make no claim to

mediumistic powers, have had striking evidence of survival. When I wrote my psychic columns for the newspapers I was sent countless stories from people who say they have left their bodies during operations, seen apparitions of dead loved ones, had correct premonitions of a family death or received communications from spirit visitors that could be verified through the Public Records.

NEAR DEATH EXPERIENCES (NDE's)

Many medical Doctors and surgeons now accept that there is a continuation of life beyond the grave.

Much of the strongest evidence comes from those who have died on the operating table and been resuscitated. Even though clinically brain dead, they have described leaving their bodies and entering, for a short period, the afterlife. Many patients have been free of drugs and have had no preconceived beliefs. Their experiences have, furthermore, been fully lucid and, unlike a dream, can be remembered in detail—which would discredit any suggestion that they are either drug-induced or created by chemical reactions in the brain

Some of the most interesting proofs of the continuation of life after death have been given by children. Dr Kübler-Ross made extensive studies of patients' reports of near death experiences from families involved in multiple-death family car accidents. She quotes many instances where dying children have known which family members have died and given the correct time of their passing.

Other cases involve adults who have claimed to have left their body and have been able to describe details of events in the operating theatre. Dr Michael Sabom describes how a US Air Force pilot, after being resuscitated from a massive heart attack, had an out of the body experience and was able to describe correctly the amounts of electricity displayed on the defibrillator even though it was completely out of the patient's view.

One blind patient described in minute detail the designs and colors of the clothing being worn by her surgeons. Another blind patient was able to give the numbers registered on the anesthetist's machinery. Another woman, whilst in this state, explained that a shoe was lodged high up on a windowsill. The shoe was found to be exactly where she had described and could not have been seen prior to its discovery.

Subjects undergoing near-death-experiences describe an afterlife that is very real and lucid. They recount seeing a tunnel of light that leads to a beautiful place where they encounter their loved ones who have gone before them: the same world that mediums, prophets and religions have been describing for centuries.

DEATH BED VISIONS OF THE FAMOUS

The philosopher, Emanuel Swedenborg, arguably the first modern medium, predicted the exact date of his death, weeks in advance. A servant girl who was present at his passing said 'He was pleased, as if he was going to have a holiday, to go on some merry-making.'

Similarly, the great British poet, William Blake, had ecstatic visions as he lay dying. His friends, who sat with him, said that Blake stared into space and drew pictures of spirit people that he saw clearly. His wife wrote 'Just before he died his countenance became fair—his eyes brightened, and he burst out in singing of the things he saw in heaven.'

The poet, Wordsworth, on the point of death, said that he saw his dead sister, Dorothy, come for him. Author, Aldous Huxley, fearlessly enhanced his experience by taking mescaline on his death bed. And Carl Jung, the famous psychiatrist, in his autobiography, 'Memories, Dreams, Reflections', describes glimpses of the afterlife and had an out-of-body-experience. "The images were so tremendous that I myself concluded that I was close to death. My nurse afterwards told me, 'It was as if you were surrounded by a bright glow.' That was a phenomenon she had sometimes observed in the dying, she added. I had reached the outermost limit, and do not know whether I was in a dream or an ecstasy. At any rate extremely strange things began to happen to me.

It seemed to me that I was high up in space. Far below I saw the globe of the earth, bathed in a gloriously blue light. I saw the deep blue sea and the continents. Far below my feet lay Ceylon, and in the distance ahead of me the subcontinent of India."

Stranger still is the deathbed vision of the Duke of Windsor on 22 May 1972. His life had been destroyed and kingship denied him because he married American divorcee Wallis Simpson. Much of the anguish had been caused by his deceased mother, Queen Mary. Yet the Duke of Windsor's dying words were 'Mama... Mama... Mama... Mama.' Had his mother forgiven him in death for those things she could never have done in life?

THE NATURE OF MEDIUMSHIP

Mediumship, the ability to communicate with the afterlife, involves three psychic skills:

CLAIRVOYANCE: The ability to see spirit images. This is normally an 'inward' seeing focused in the third eye center. The medium sees pictures and images that relate to the spirit communicators life.

CLAIRSENTIENCE: The ability to sense spirit presence. The medium senses the gender and bodily conditions of the passing associated with the spirit communicator.

CLAIRAUDIENCE: The ability to hear spirit voices. Described simply by the medium Doris Stokes as 'voices in my ear', the sounds are in reality more like an inner voice. The throat center is considered the chakra through which this ability activates.

TYPES OF MEDIUMSHIP:

There are also various types of mediumship:

INSPIRATIONAL: The medium talks on a chosen spiritual subject and feels his words influenced by guiding spirit people.

MENTAL: The medium senses, sees and hears the spirit communicator and repeats the information he is given.

TRANCE: The spirit communicator talks directly through the medium using his voice box.

PHYSICAL: An entranced medium, sitting in a darkened room, exudes a white, luminous misty substance called ectoplasm. This mist solidifies into spirit people that are as real as the séance members. Sometimes a rod of ectoplasm is formed that allows a spirit to talk through a 'trumpet'.

TRANSFIGURATION: Ectoplasm forms only over the entranced medium's face. The superimposed face of the spirit communicator is seen by the participants.

DIRECT VOICE: Mediums like Leslie Flint evolved an artificial voice box formed from ectoplasm. The spirit voice is disembodied and can be heard coming from different parts of the room.

THE OBJECTIVES OF SPIRIT COMMUNICATION

The objective of mediumship is to prove survival of the human personality after bodily death, which is a simple goal but has gigantic philosophical implications. Mediumship is not fortune telling. Those that wish to develop mediumship for egotistical reasons should stop now. Some aspirants desire to be publically admired and be worshiped as the great mystic. This is the wrong approach. You must have an inner yearning to serve a higher purpose. You are a humble servant of the good.

It is not an easy path: you will encounter ridicule and opposition from the ignorant. You may even encounter aggression from extremist Christian sects that believe all psychic skills are the work of the Devil. The development of mediumship brings with it the need to find Truth. Once you've found it, through spirit proof, nothing can shake you from the path.

A HELPING HAND

It can take many years of patiently sitting, before physical mediumship develops. Trance also requires many years to perfect. Both require a well-structured circle and readers are advised not to practice these skills without supervision by a developed medium.

We're going to concentrate on how to develop Mental Mediumship. It's better to practice with others as within a circle there is lots of auric energy that can be used to help develop you. And, if your motives are sincere and not neurotic or fearful, you won't attract any undesirable spirits to disrupt you.

DEVELOPING MEDIUMSHIP

You, the aspiring medium, are like a computer and the spirit world supplies the program and information. You can't force mediumship. It is primarily a passive state of consciousness in which your mind is open and receptive. You will receive impressions and thoughts and, if you want your communications to be clear and accurate, you must quieten the mind.

Before a medium starts they usually spend about half an hour in quiet meditation to allow the mind to become still and open to the impressions coming from spirit. Most mediums also open aura by running spiritual energy through the centers in the spirit body called the chakras. I have not explained how to do this here but for many people the chakras will open in meditation naturally and without their realizing it. During meditation the breath will become quiet and the spirit people can come close. All is completely under your control and the spirit people will never push you further than you are prepared to go.

Once you've opened your aura, either through a specific visualization technique or by letting it happen spontaneously during meditation, you enter silent meditation and then send out thoughts asking the spirit people to draw close. The link with spirit is made through the power of love. You may feel the presence of people, whom you know in the spirit, draw close, or you may see colored lights and visual images. Some people just feel calm and peaceful within.

Don't expect suddenly to see spirit forms or hear voices. The bridge between the two worlds is built slowly. Note the things you see, and describe them to the others who sit with you when the period of deep meditation is over.

You will need to sit regularly with others once a week at the same time and on the same day. The spirit people will be aware that you are attempting to develop mediumship and will draw close to help. They will understand the level of your development and won't frighten you or push you too far. They won't push you into a trance. If you feel yourself wanting to slip off into trance, I would suggest that in the early stages you resist. A good medium perfects mental mediumship first. You are the one who is always in control of your gift. Trance can come much later, once you've fully developed your mediumistic gift over a number of years.

SPIRIT GUIDES

Each of us has a guardian angel who is a spirit person that protects us and guides the progress of our soul. Some have argued that these 'guides' are figments of the imagination and draw parallels with psychiatric cases of multiple personality. The early Spiritualists went to great lengths to disprove this. One famous American Indian spirit communicator named 'Silver Birch', who worked through the mediumship of Maurice Barbanell, suggested a way to quantify his reality and to do this he spoke the exact words as he had communicated in his circle at other séances. At the circle of Estelle Roberts the spirit spoke the message through a trumpet and again at another meeting through the mediumship of Nena Mayer. This continued until Maurice Barbanell and his circle were convinced that Silver Birch was indeed an independent being.

Similar empirical proofs have been given through other great trance teachers. Whether these teachers are in reality American Indians, Chinamen, Zulus etc. is another question. Some 'guides' have suggested that they take on a form that can easily be recognized by the medium and the people sitting in the séances. As they have progressed into the higher planes of the afterlife, it seems reasonable that they should shed their earthly form. They have become 'beings of light' and manifest as people from exotic cultures when they link with the earth plane. In this way we recognize our teachers.

LINKING-UP WITH YOUR SPIRITUAL GUIDE

Your initial spirit impressions will come to you while you're sitting in meditation. Your main spirit guide—known by some as 'the doorkeeper'—will draw close. You will 'feel' their presence. You may feel spiritual emotions and begin to feel them helping you with your inner problems and thoughts. Spirit communication is a blending of your consciousness with that of spirit. Your mind won't become a blank; nor will you be taken over. At all times you will be conscious and in control.

Gradually you will begin to get to know your guide. Other helpers will also draw close. The various guides have different functions. Some may help you with healing; others are there to teach; some aid with communication and there are even guides to make you laugh. As you progress you will get to know them like long lost friends.

MEDIUMISTIC COMMUNICATION

A time will come when you feel confident enough to make a spirit communication for someone. The spirit people will teach you your own style of working. Every medium is different and there are as many ways of working as there are different human personalities. However, there are a few basic aids to clear communication:

Firstly you need to 'link' to your sitter. Ask them to say a few words. The sound of the voice establishes a vibrational link between them and you. In the early stages it's best to start on a psychic level and then progress to mediumship. Initially you link with the person's aura, which in some ways is a little like the idea of linking to the other person's subconscious mind, as I showed you in relation to how to use your intuition. The blending of the aura happens naturally and I have explained how to do this consciously in my other books. When you feel spiritually connected, start by telling the sitter a few things about their personality, present life and past. As the psychic bond between you builds, turn to your inner impressions and ask, in your mind, for the spirit people to give you some information through your intuition.

The best mediums are in control of their communication. A mental conversation is held with the spirit person. So ask questions inwardly and, most importantly, listen to the reply. The answers to your questions may not necessarily come back as words but you may get feeling, thought, impressions, associated personal memories, a song... the spirit will use every way they can muster to get the information you need into your head. The more you interfere with the incoming impressions the more distorted your evidence becomes. Let the spirit people do the work but push the communicator to give evidence. The guides will bring the communicator forward but you must encourage them to speak.

Here's a few hints on building a psychic bridge between the two worlds. As you progress you will probably establish your own way of working but, whatever your method, try to establish structure to your communication.

1. In your mind ask the spirit communicator what gender they are. (Clairsentience is the easiest information to obtain.) Relay your information to your sitter: "I have a lady with me."

2. Ask the spirit communicator to show you their size and again say what you feel: "It's a big cuddly lady"

3. Ask if they're family, friend or acquaintance: "This is a family member. I feel a motherly vibration. I believe I'm with your grandmother on your mother's side of the family."

4. Ask about their passing. Was it quick or slow? What illnesses did they have? How did they pass? "This lady suffered with her back through life. She had long term stomach problems but she passed quickly with a heart attack." You will feel the

communicator's earthly physical conditions superimposed on your own body. If you feel uncomfortable ask the spirit communicator to take the condition away. Of course, the spirit person no longer suffers as she did on earth but the conditions of their passing are a powerful part of the proof.

5. Now ask about their personality. Were they a happy person? Are there any unusual character traits? Were they stubborn or easy going? In your own mind you will feel like the person, as their thoughts overlay with your own. "Your Grandmother could really dig her heals in. She was bossy and liked to push Grandad around." Tell the sitter as many things as you can about their Grandmother's personality. Build a character profile in the same way as you did in the chapter on psychometry. This time you're not reading an object as you did with psychometry: you're reading a real spirit person.

WHAT YOU'VE DONE

So far in the reading you've used the psychic gift of clairsentience. You've felt the gender, form, illnesses and personality of the spirit person. You've used the skills you learnt through psychometry but in a more advanced way. The next step is to use clairvoyance—to see pictures and images:

6. Ask the communicator to impress visions into your third eye center, in the center of the forehead, and relay what you see. Again don't censor your thoughts. For example: "I see a lion". The sitter looks perplexed. "A Red Lion—did she work at a pub called the Red Lion?" The images have a meaning. At first you may misunderstand them or confuse them with your own thoughts but, if you keep asking the spirit communicator to expand the image, you'll understand the message they are trying to convey. Sometimes, your subconscious may turn the spirits thoughts into symbols: interpret these as you learnt in the chapter on dreams.

Many mediums never progress beyond the levels of Clairsentience or Clairvoyance yet their spirit proof can be quite accurate. At first, Clairaudience—hearing the spirit—comes slowly. Although the 'voice' may appear to come from the ear, in reality it comes from the mind. Only in physical mediumship can other people hear the voice. Clairaudience is a subjective experience; a blending of consciousness.

7. If words come to you, say them. Again you may at first only get part of the information. "I hear the word Devon." The sitter says she has no connection with Devon. "No it's not Devon it's Devonshire. Do you understand Devonshire?" The sitter may then understand this. It was her Grandmother's maiden name.

At first you may not get all the names right. Clairaudience is an advanced form of mediumship and, in my opinion, may be inherently difficult to achieve because mediumship uses the non-verbal right hand side of the brain. However, try constantly to progress towards it even if sometimes you make embarrassing mistakes. The information you are receiving from spirit is correct but your own subconscious thoughts have got in the way.

Perfected clairaudience is remarkable. In time you may not only be able to give the first and second name of the communicator but give their address and telephone number as well. All mediums find this type of information difficult to pick up. But it's possible and sooner or later, if you work hard and discipline yourself, you'll get there.

YOU MAY ALSO ENJOY THESE BOOKS BY CRAIG HAMILTON-PARKER

BUY FROM PSYCHICS.CO.UK

MESSAGES FROM THE UNIVERSE

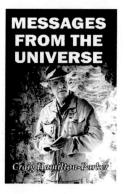

The incredible story of Craig's encounter with the Naadi Oracle of India and how it predicts the future with 100% accuracy – including the future day of his death. Craig tells the story of his encounter with the oracle and writes about the implications of fate and destiny. The book also tells of Craig and his wife Jane's work as a mediumistic couple and how they travel the world giving readings to celebrities and meet holy people as they fulfil the startling predictions made by the oracle.

WHAT TO DO WHEN YOU ARE DEAD

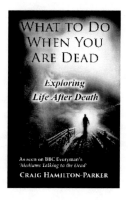

"What to Do When You Are Dead is a landmark book" – Psychic News

Is there life after death? In this book Craig draws on cross cultural beliefs and his own work to describe what life is like in the afterlife. This book will help you to overcome the fear of death and prepare you for the next-life. Based on extensive research and direct insights the book builds a picture of what the afterlife is like and what life is like on the other side.

PSYCHIC SCHOOL: HOW TO BECOME A PSYCHIC MEDIUM

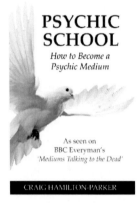

Filmed over a year in a three part documentary for the BBC, Craig and Jane Hamilton-Parker's psychic students were taught from novices to become mediums capable of working in a theatre. This book expands on the lessons seen in the programs with additional teachings from Craig's thirty years of mediumship. It takes you step-by-step from developing basic psychic powers to becoming a professional medium.

PSYCHIC PROTECTION – SAFE MEDIUMSHIP

If you are a psychic medium or someone who is very sensitive to spiritual vibrations, you may be influenced by the positive or negative energies around you.

Through examples from Craig and Jane's files he explains how to combat negative influences, work safely with ghosts, poltergeists, spells and spirits and how to protect your spiritual journey.

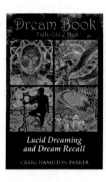
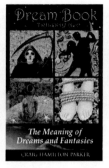

THE DREAM BOOK TRILOGY

Read all three books in this series. In *Lucid Dreaming and Dream Recall* you are shown how to bring your dreams to life and eventually become a lucid dreamer with the ability to wake up in a dream as it is taking place. In the *Meaning of Dreams and Fantasies* you will learn to interpret and understand your dreams and fantasies. *Mystical Dream Interpretation* explains your psychic dreams and dreams about the future.

ORDER BOOKS AT:
psychics.co.uk or Amazon

PSYCHIC & MEDIUMISTIC
READING SERVICES

Craig & Jane Hamilton-Parker offer psychic and mediumistic readings from their website. They also have an online community where you can ask questions and share your paranormal dreams and psychic insights with like-minded people.

Visit: psychics.co.uk

If you would like a reading today you can call their telephone psychics and book a reading on the numbers below:

UK: 0800 067 8600
USA: 1855 444 6887
EIRE: 1800 719 656
AUSTRALIA: 1800 825 305

ABOUT THE AUTHOR

 **Craig Hamilton-Parker** is a British author, television personality and professional psychic medium. He is best known for his TV shows *Our Psychic Family*, *The Spirit of Diana* and *Nightmares Decoded*. On television he usually works with his wife Jane Hamilton-Parker who is also a psychic medium. Their work was showcased in a three part documentary on the BBC called *Mediums Talking to the Dead*.

They now have TV shows in the USA and spend a lot of time demonstrating mediumship around the world.

Born in Southampton UK, Craig was convinced at an early age that he was mediumistic. He became a well-known as a platform medium within Spiritualism and in 1994 left his job as advertising executive to become the resident psychic on Channel 4 television's *The Big Breakfast* making predictions for upcoming news stories. He wrote a regular psychic advice column for *The Scottish Daily Record* and regular features for *The Daily Mail*, *Sunday Mirror* and *The People*.

His first book about the psychic genre was published in 1995 and are now published in many languages. You can find out more and join Craig & Jane's work and Spiritual Foundation at their website: **psychics.co.uk**

Manufactured by Amazon.ca
Acheson, AB

10860597R00098